To

_____

From

_____

Date

_____

D0829939

**ON THE GO FAMILY DEVOTION**

# FIRST STEPS TOGETHER
# TOGETHER
## Family Devotional

## FOR FAMILIES WITH BABIES AND TODDLERS AGES 0-2

MATT AND NOEL
GUEVARA

An imprint of Rose Publishing, Inc.
Carson, CA
www.Rose-Publishing.com

**ON THE GO: FAMILY DEVOTION**
**FIRST STEPS TOGETHER – FAMILY DEVOTIONAL**
© 2016 Matt and Noel Guevara

RoseKidz®
An imprint of Rose Publishing, Inc.®
17909 Adria Maru Lane
Carson, CA 90746
www.Rose-Publishing.com

Register your book at www.Rose-Publishing.com/register. Get inspiration via email, sign up at www.Rose-Publishing.com.

Unless otherwise indicated, Scripture quotations are taken from the New International Reader's Version of the Bible, Copyright © 1995, 1996, 1998, 2014 by Biblica, Inc.® Used by permission. All rights reserved worldwide.

Verses marked NIV are taken from the New International Version (NIV) Holy Bible, New International Version®, NIV® Copyright © 1973, 1978, 1984, 2011 by Biblica, Inc.® Used by permission. All rights reserved worldwide.

*Cover and interior design by Nancy L. Haskins*
*Cover photo by Nadya Eugene*
*Animal illustrations by Pushnova*

ISBN 10: 1-628625-00-7
ISBN 13: 978-1-628625-00-4
RoseKidz® reorder #L50005
RELIGION/Christian Ministry/Children

## DEDICATION

This book is dedicated to our parents:
Bob and Cindy Denen
Michael and Susan Guevara

We are filled with gratitude for your incredible wisdom, patience, persistence, and love. But your greatest gifts have been to talk to us about Jesus every day and to follow God in front of us for a lifetime.

## NICE WORDS ABOUT FIRST STEPS

"It seems like in life we get the least training for our most important missions in life. If you have ever felt overwhelmed when it comes to bringing Christ into the everyday life of your family, then this incredible book by Noel and Matt is your lifeline. You don't need to know it all at once, just use these devotionals one week at a time! You and your kids will be blessed."

– David Wakerley, *Hillsong Kids* Pastor
and Creative Director

"There are so many resources for parents of infants and toddlers … but finally we have a resource that helps parents spiritually through this crucial stage. I can't think of anyone better than Matt and Noel to lead parents on that journey…" – Jeremy Lee, Founder, *ParentMinistry*

"Like tons of parents, I didn't start getting serious about my faith until I had kids. And it took a while. But if I had this wonderfully do-able devotional by Matt and Noel Guevara, I would have plugged into the power of God and His Word much sooner. Plus, it has parenting tips. Plus, ways to engage your children's faith. Plus, it's really funny!"

– Jay Payleitner, speaker and best selling author
of *52 Things Kids Need from a Dad*

# Table of Contents

## Part 3: Ascent: Responding to the Holy Spirit

## Part 4: Break Trail: Charting Spiritual Disciplines

# Introduction

The greatest journeys make for the greatest stories. Think of the classic childhood stories you enjoyed in your younger years. Goldilocks, on a personal journey, finds the home of the Three Bears in the trees. Peter Pan whisks Wendy, John, and Michael away to Neverland to battle Captain Hook. Max travels "in and out of weeks and through a year" to *Where the Wild Things Are.* In *The Lion, The Witch and The Wardrobe,* four siblings named Peter, Susan, Edmund, and Lucy Pevensie are evacuated from London during World War II. A game of hide-and-seek leads Lucy through the wardrobe into the land of Narnia. We bought the complete *Chronicles of Narnia* as a gift before our first child was born. Over the years, we have read these journeys out loud to our four children and other children we have welcomed into our home.

While some journeys connect us to places, other journeys connect us to people – some who join us on our journey for a season, and some who come alongside as we embark on the journey of a lifetime. Our (Matt and Noel's) paths first crossed in elementary school, and by middle school we had already decided that we were meant to walk hand in hand – literally and figuratively – for the rest of our lives. We navigated adolescence together and entered adulthood eager to start a family of our own. While our journey has had its ups and downs, moments of celebration and seasons of heartbreak, we have been intentional in partnering with each other as we follow Christ. That partnership is most evident as we parent our four children.

For better or worse, we hit the road each day, with varying degrees of success and failure. Good days go something like this: our daughters' small group leader at church pulls us aside to let us know that during worship, our girls (both tweens) often hold hands and raise their free hands to praise their heavenly Father. Bad days go something like this: we distribute Chinese take out and our son Zion, who is three years old, looks at us both and states, "I want a new mom and dad." So we send him to his room and ration his Orange Chicken. We are blessed to be on this journey together, and while we don't always agree on everything, we are intentional about sharing God's Story with our children. We create space to pass on our faith, because someday we pray that they will continue their spiritual journey, prepared to pass their faith on to the next generation.

Through the pages of this book, instead of walking through the wardrobe into the world of Narnia, we will walk into the story of Scripture by examining 52 different passages gathered around four themes. Over the next 52 weeks, we invite you to join us on the journey. We'll be transparent about our weaknesses, in hopes that you can relate to the struggles we all face as parents. We'll turn to God's Word, knowing that his strength is made perfect in our weakness. And we'll prompt you to share your faith with your child, believing that now is the best time to prepare them for the spiritual journey ahead. Here's what the journey ahead will entail...

# TRAIL MAP:
## Knowing God

We begin the journey by studying some of God's key attributes. Getting to know God's character is a lifelong journey, and it plots the course for our spiritual growth. As you learn more about who God is, you will grow in your own faith, and will construct a framework for spiritually parenting your children. The attributes we chose to write about are not all inclusive, or ranked in order of importance. We encourage you to continue your journey to know God, reading his Word each day with a heart eager to learn how he reveals himself throughout Scripture. Our God wants to be known by you, and as you seek to know him he will reveal himself to you through his Word and throughout his Story.

# COMPASS:
## Navigating God's Story

We continue the journey by investigating what God has done through the unified story in his Word. The Bible is not a collection of stories about people. It is one story about God, a complete narrative that includes people and places and things that help us understand who God is and what he has done. As you understand God and his unfolding plan, you can orient yourself to your place in his greater Story. This Story is meant to help you navigate your own child's story and faith development.

## SECTION THREE

# ASCENT:
## *Responding to the Holy Spirit*

We continue moving along the journey by focusing on the work of the Holy Spirit, and our practical response. This part of the journey offers unique challenges, as it requires us to take careful and deliberate steps to listen to the Spirit's direction and respond. When we as parents learn to respond to the Holy Spirit, we are better able to partner with him in raising our children, coming alongside of the work he is doing in their hearts. By depending on the Holy Spirit throughout our parenting journey, we join with God in the hard work of parenting and growth.

## SECTION FOUR

# BREAK TRAIL:
## *Charting Spiritual Disciplines*

We end this part of the journey by outlining key spiritual disciplines that we as parents must model for our children. Our children will respond naturally to God, but as beginners on their spiritual journey, we make the uncharted path easier to travel by going ahead, leaving footsteps for them to walk in. As we create these rhythms, they will establish foundations for a lifetime.

Throughout each devotional you will develop a rhythm for growing in your own faith and then passing on your faith to your child. Each of the 52 devotionals, intended to be completed one week at a time over the course of a year, will provide an opportunity for you to spiritually parent your child in a simple but meaningful way. There are four elements to each weekly devotional:

## MEDITATE

Passage of Scripture to read and respond to. This will include a key passage of one or two verses, as well as a suggested extended passage for further study. Take time to not only read this passage each week, but also meditate on it, so its words will take root in your heart.

## ANTICIPATE

Reflection questions to help set the tone for the journey. These simple questions will prepare your heart and focus your thoughts so can prepare to fully engage with God and your child. Take a few moments to reflect on these questions, examining your heart and answering transparently.

## RELATE

Honest stories from our parenting experiences, good and bad. These stories will remind you that we are all on this journey together. Oftentimes we compare ourselves with other parents at their best moment and feel ill equipped for the journey ahead. Other times we witness setbacks and families who have lost their way and we worry that we don't stand a chance on such a narrow road. By sharing each other's stories and viewing them in the light of God's Word, we can find encouragement that we are not alone on the journey, and that together we can spur each other along the way.

An engaging application of the week's study for you to do with your child. There are twelve unique types of activities, designed to engage a variety of learning styles and interests. These activities are integrated throughout the year and provide an opportunity for you to bond with your child as you introduce them to faith.

They offer a simple but tangible way for you to bring your child along with you on your spiritual journey.

## BABY *Steps* and TODDLER *Steps*

These unique touch point activities called Baby Steps and Toddler Steps offer a unique response to each passage designed just for their developmental level. You will grow to find that passing on your faith can and should be seamlessly woven into your daily rhythms and routines.

The greatest journeys make for the greatest stories. We invite you now to begin moving toward knowing God deeply, responding to his Spirit intimately, and leading your children confidently. What might God accomplish in your life over the next 52 weeks?

# God is Present

## MEDITATE

*"LORD, even before I speak a word, you know all about it. You are all around me, behind me and in front of me. You hold me, in your safe hand."* – Psalm 139:4-5

Extended passage: Psalms 139

## ANTICIPATE

● How does your child request (or demand!) your presence?

_____

_____

● When or where have you needed God's presence this week?

_____

_____

_____

My firstborn had the hardest time transitioning from womb to world. I spent hours rocking and holding Isabel, afraid to move as she dozed off with her head resting on my shoulder. As she grew, those hours were spent sitting next to her crib, because she would only fall asleep if she knew I was there. She loved to hold onto my finger, so I spent hours contorted in the car or walking next to her in the stroller with my arm awkwardly stretched out to reach her chubby toddler hands. I wanted Isabel to know I was with her. Only sometimes I couldn't be, and those times were hard on my brand new mama heart. Eventually I had to let her sleep in her room alone, leave her in the church nursery, drop her off with a babysitter while I went to work.

## LETTING GO

Our babies spend nine months with their mothers all around them. And then from the moment they enter the world, we begin readying them to head out on their own without us. It's a huge undertaking, preparing these sweet little ones to become everything God created them to be. And oftentimes this responsibility is overwhelming. But we can take comfort in knowing that at all times and in all things, God is all around us. He is behind us, in the preparing us for this moment. He is in front of us, in the working of all things for our good (and maybe even smoothing out our mistakes). And he holds us in his power, with even greater care and comfort than we hold our own little ones.

## NEVER ALONE

The even better news is that we can root our children in this reality. Even when we cannot be with them, our children are never alone. Before they ever speak a word, God knows all about it. God is all around them - behind and in front of them - holding them close so they are always in his presence. Take comfort in God's presence today, and begin teaching your little one to do the same.

# BABY

Babies love to listen to their parents' voices, picking up on inflections and eventually simple words and phrases; they are able to comprehend much more than they can speak. Take time this week to give your child the gift of your presence. Put away your phone and other distractions. Sit with your little one in a peaceful place and let them know with words and actions that you enjoy being with them. As you impress on their hearts that you enjoy being present with them, you are tilling the soil to grow the truth that God loves to be present with them always. Read Psalm 139:4-5 aloud. Ask: who is always with you? And answer: God is always with you! Repeat this question and answer throughout the week whenever you have to leave your child – at bedtime, when you drop them off at a sitters, or when you head out to run errands. Pray that they will find peace and comfort in God's loving presence.

BABY

We can take comfort in knowing that at all times and in all things, God is all around us.

## TODDLER *Tips*

Take comfort in God's presence today, and begin teaching your little one to do the same.

# TODDLER *Steps*

Toddlers learn new words and phrases by repeating what they've heard, and they love spending time with their parents. Take time this week to give your child the gift of your presence, free from all distractions. Sit with your little toddler in a peaceful place and spend time doing something he or she enjoys – rock them a little longer, tell them one more story, or sing an extra lullaby. As you impress on their hearts that you enjoy being present with them, you are tilling the soil to grow the truth that God loves to be present with them always.

Read Psalm 139:4-5 aloud. Ask: who is always with you? And have your toddler repeat after you: God! Repeat the question and answer a few times until your toddler catches on. Continue asking this question throughout the week, and soon they'll be able to answer on their own.

# CHAPTER 2

# God is Love

## 📖 MEDITATE

*"Dear friends, let us love one another, because love comes from God. Anyone who loves has become a child of God and knows God. Anyone who does not love does not know God, because God is love."*

– 1 John 4:7-8

Extended passage: 1 John 4:7-12

## ✏️ ANTICIPATE

● How would you describe the love your dad had for you as a child?

_____

_____

_____

● How would you describe God's love for you?

_____

_____

_____

## RELATE

Ask most dads – we all remember the first time we laid eyes on our newborn child. I will never forget the moment when our firstborn Isabel was placed in my arms. A tumultuous twenty-hour delivery ended in my wife being taken for emergency surgery. Doctors and nurses filled the delivery room while I nervously pulled scrubs over my clothes. In the operating room, I had no idea what to expect as I gripped my wife's hand. Moments later, I was handed a tiny person wrapped in a hospital blanket and for the first time I saw her face, touched her skin, heard her cries. From that moment I knew: this child was mine. And my heart was filled with love. I was so enraptured in her beauty that when the nurse asked me for my baby's name, I told her the wrong one! Don't worry, I fixed it before my wife found out.

## GOD IS LOVE

Many times I look down on love, thinking that love is too emotional, too wishy-washy and touchy-feely. The "loving" parent should be my wife Noel and as a dad, I should embody something different for my children. Endurance. Persistence. Work Ethic. MacGuyver. Rocky Balboa. A Superhero. You know, man stuff. But then I began to think about 1 John 4:8 and noticed two things. First, the word "love" is not a verb. Did you catch that? The word "love" does not describe what God does, it is a noun defining who God is.
God IS love (emphasis mine).

## BE AN EXAMPLE

Second, the word love is applied to God himself. If the same God who was called the Lion of Judah, who formed the cosmos with the sound of his voice, and crafted man and woman by hand out of the dirt IS love. I can follow his example of love for my kids, especially in their early years. As a parent, you embody love for your child just as your heavenly Father embodies love for you. As a mom or dad, you set the framework for how your children understand and know love, especially as babies and toddlers.

Photo © Hannamariah

# BABY *Steps*

Babies need love and affection as much as they need food, warmth, and shelter. This week, take time to demonstrate love to your child as you practice the biblical concept of consecration. While not part of our modern day rhythms, times of consecration were initiated in Bible times to create holy moments, set apart as sacred, dedicated to a divine purpose. Meet your baby's need for love and affection in tangible ways with eye contact, words of affirmation and a strong hug.

Hold them close and whisper this prayer of consecration: Little child in my arms, I am your dad/mom. I love you. My love for you cannot be broken – not by what you say or how you act. My love for you is strong. May you know my deep, resounding love over you all the days of your life, especially in the times I fail to demonstrate it for you. And may the love of your heavenly Father be your strength. Amen.

## BABY *Bite*

The word "love" does not describe what God does, it is a noun defining who God is. God IS love.

TODDLER *Tips*

As a mom or dad, you set
the framework for how your
children understand and
know love, especially as
babies and toddlers.

# TODDLER *Steps*

Toddlers continue to need love and affection and are
also beginning to respond in kind. Take time this week
to demonstrate love to your child as you lead them in a
prayer of consecration – time initiated to create a holy
moment, sacred and dedicated to God.

   As you hold them close, look them in the eyes and invite
them to snuggle in and pray with you: My child, I want you
to know something that will never, ever change. I am your
father/mother and I love you. Just like I am holding you up
in my arms, my love will hold you up every day of your life.
You can always know that I love you. But God's strong love
for you is even greater. Your heavenly Father God loves
you more than you could ever imagine. I pray you will
know this love each day. Amen.

# CHAPTER 3

# God is Our Comforter

## MEDITATE

*"...who comforts us in all our troubles, so that we can comfort those in any trouble with the comfort that we ourselves receive from God."*
— 2 Corinthians 1:4 (NIV)

Extended passage: 2 Corinthians 2:1-11

## ANTICIPATE

● What is your child's favorite comfort item or routine?

_____

_____

_____

● What reminds you of God and gives you comfort? (A verse? Place? Line from a song?)

_____

_____

## ♥ RELATE

I expected motherhood to come naturally to me. I remember being pregnant and standing in the doorway of the nursery, imagining the time I would spend rocking a cooing baby before putting her peacefully to sleep. But then my birth plan fell apart, as they often do, and I began my motherhood journey recovering from a caesarian section and a host of complications, with a colicky baby that screamed more often than she cooed and didn't drift peacefully to sleep for many months.

### REALITY CHECK

I found myself floundering in my attempts to care for and comfort Isabel, and then her sister Sofia, who arrived 13 months later. As surprised as I was at how difficult motherhood was, I was even more surprised at how deeply I could love these tiny bundles, and how my heart ached to respond to each and every one of their cries. But at the end of long days and in the middle of longer nights, I found my well of comfort running dry. Paul reminds us here in 2 Corinthians 1 that God comforts us in all of our troubles.

### TAKE COMFORT

What are you struggling with as a parent today? Maybe, like me, you're feeling guilty that this isn't coming more naturally to you. Perhaps you're having a hard time balancing your new role with a host of other demands. Know that God longs to comfort you. As God comforts us, we can comfort others. Whether you have an easy newborn, a fussy, teething baby, or a spirited toddler, they need a great deal of comfort, even when your well may seem to run dry. Take heart in knowing that you don't need to muster the comfort your child requires on your own. Draw from the well that your heavenly Father promises to keep filled to overflowing. Draw from that well during middle of the night feedings and in the midst of nap strikes and during those bouts with the flu. Then, once comforted, turn and share God's comfort with your child.

Photo © DONOT6_STUDIO

# BABY *Steps*

Babies love to listen to music and enjoy the sound of their parents' voices, and music has a calming and comforting effect on them. Turn on a favorite song that encourages you to appreciate who God is, and receive his comfort. I love the hymn "His Eye Is on the Sparrow," but feel free to choose whatever song will remind you that God is your Comforter. Share your troubles with your heavenly Father, rest in his presence, and appreciate him for being a heavenly Father who comforts you in all of your troubles. Then snuggle up with your baby on your lap and grab a soft blanket or favorite comfort item and hold them as you sing along with the song. Play the song throughout the week to remind you and your child of God's comfort.

## BABY *Bite*

Take heart in knowing that you don't need to muster the comfort your child requires on your own. Draw from the well that your heavenly Father promises to keep filled to overflowing.

# TODDLER *Steps*

Toddlers love music and often show it by bouncing, clapping their hands, or dancing. Some toddlers are ready to start singing along. Turn on a favorite song that will encourage you appreciate God as your Comforter. Give God your burdens, rest in his presence and appreciate your heavenly Father who comforts you in all of your troubles. Encourage your toddler to move to the beat and join you in singing the song, or rock them while holding a favorite comfort item. Play the song throughout the week to remind you and your child of God's comfort.

# CHAPTER 4

# God is Our Deliverer

## 📖 MEDITATE

*David sang to the LORD the words of this song when the LORD delivered him from the hand of all his enemies and from the hand of Saul. He said: "The LORD is my rock, my fortress and my deliverer..."*

— 2 Samuel 22:1-2 (NIV)

Extended passage: 2 Samuel 22:1-51

## ✏️ ANTICIPATE

● Growing up did you have a place you loved to hide in? Where was it?

_____

_____

_____

● What's the best pillow fort you have ever made?

_____

_____

_____

My dad and mom came from completely unique family experiences. My father's dad died when he was an infant and he was raised as an only child by his mom and aunt. My mother has eleven brothers and sisters. Her mother had over 80 grandchildren and over 120 great grandchildren. My family was always going to a hospital to welcome a new baby into the family. I did not particularly enjoy these trips because two things would happen. First, I would be asked if I wanted to hold the baby (I would always say, "Yes"). Second, the moment the baby touched my arms no less than 50 people started critiquing the way I was holding the child.

"Put your elbow up." "Put your elbow down."

"Hold her neck." "Support her back."

## HOLD THE BABY

As a result, I was absolutely terrified when we had our first child. I was afraid I would not know how to hold her correctly. This fear was magnified a thousand times when the doctors had to deliver the baby through emergency surgery. Instead of my wife holding our daughter first, it would be up to me. For sure, I was going to break her and fifty family members would remind me of my poor baby holding techniques from childhood.

## CARE

These stories make me chuckle, especially when I read David's song in 2 Samuel 22. David sings these words to God, "The LORD is my rock, my fortress and my deliverer…" The truth is God takes care of us even when we expect him not to. There are moments in our lives as we look at the baby in our arms or walk hand in hand with our toddler, we do not expect to win – the situation around us may seem dire, finances may be tight, relationships strained, work stressful. God takes care of us anyway. David knew he was safe in God's hands and today, we can trust our child in God's hands. He will always deliver them.

Photo © Zachary Haskins

# BABY *Steps*

It can be a little nerve wracking to trust our baby in the hands of another person. Have you ever handed your baby to a young niece or nephew? But this week, as you hand your child to another person, remember David's words.

Write your own song of praise to God. Use 2 Samuel 22 as your guide. Fill in the blanks:

God is my _____, my _____ and _____.

Write this simple psalm down and place it in a convenient spot so you can return to it throughout the week.

## BABY *Bite*

The truth is God takes care of us even when we expect him not to.

## TODDLER *Tips*

There are moments in our lives as we look at the baby in our arms or walk hand in hand with our toddler and we do not expect to win - the situation around us may seem dire, finances may be tight, relationships strained, work stressful. God takes care of us anyway.

# TODDLER *Steps*

Transitions between parents and other caregivers can be difficult for toddlers. To help with transitions, write a song of praise to God. Use 2 Samuel 22 as your guide.

Have your toddler help you decide what to put in the blanks:

God is my _____, my _____ and _____.

Give your child some options and talk about what those options mean. (Deliverer means God helps us when we are in trouble. Rock means a strong place I can lean on.) When you fill in the blanks, have your child say the song of praise with you and rehearse it throughout the week during times of transition.

# CHAPTER 5

# God is Our Hiding Place

## 📖 MEDITATE

*"You are my hiding place. You will keep me safe from trouble. You will surround me with songs sung by those who praise you because you save your people."* – Psalm 32:7

Extended passage: Psalm 32

## ✏️ ANTICIPATE

● What are some signs that your child is overwhelmed?

_____

_____

_____

● How do you respond when you feel overwhelmed?

_____

_____

_____

Isabel was my snuggliest baby. She was my firstborn, so I probably contributed to her disdain for being put down by holding her all of the time, but she was most content swaddled tight and resting with her head close to my heart. When the sights, sounds, and feelings of the world all around became overwhelming, I would block them out for her with my arms tight around her and my voice whispering in her ear. Those were sweet moments, but they were often hard moments, too, as sometimes she would cry inconsolably for hours.

## ESCAPE HATCH

I can clearly remember one night, sitting on the couch with Isabel, both of our faces tear-stained, both of our hearts pounding, both of our bodies weary. I was completely overwhelmed, sure that my inability to comfort my own baby was a sign that I wasn't going to be a good mom. In that moment, I just wanted to run and hide. Do you ever have that feeling? Like you just want to escape and take a break from the troubles you are facing? In a culture that promotes independence and a "Can Do" spirit, hiding seems a lot like failing.

## HIDING PLACE

But the psalmist tells us different: "You are my hiding place." Sometimes on the journey, the sights, sounds, and feelings of the world all around become overwhelming. In these moments, we can take a cue from our little ones and seek safety in a Hiding Place. Maybe we need to step off the path, take a moment in God's presence, and allow his Spirit to whisper his Word in our ear. Maybe we need a season tucked away, letting him keep us safe from troubles. I love the last part of this verse: "You will surround me with songs sung by those who praise you." In moments where I am overwhelmed, I find that listening to worship music gives rest to my weary soul. This week, take notice of times when you feel overwhelmed. Seek God as your Hiding Place, trust him to keep you safe from trouble, surround yourself with songs sung by those who praise God.

Photo © BlueOrange Studio

# BABY *Steps*

Babies often give cues when they are overstimulated or overwhelmed by their environment. They may begin by staring into space, then turn away from you, begin panting, move their arms and legs more rapidly, and finally erupt into tears. When this happens, become your baby's hiding place. Scoop them up in your arms, and carry them to a calm, quiet place where they will not be overwhelmed. Tell them that they are safe and loved, and that their heavenly Father will always be their Hiding Place

### BABY *Bite*

Sometimes on the journey, the sights and sounds and feelings of the world all around become overwhelming. In these moments, we can take a cue from our little ones and seek safety in a Hiding Place.

## TODDLER *Tips*

Seek God as your Hiding
Place, trust him to keep you
safe from trouble, surround
yourself with songs sung by
those who praise God.

# TODDLER *Steps*

Toddlers also give cues when they are overstimulated, and typically those cues erupt with force! They may hit, cry, or throw their bodies on the floor in a full blown tantrum. Using a soft, reassuring voice, let them know that you understand that they are overwhelmed – that the room is too loud, their bodies are too excited, or their eyes have too much to look at. Then tell them that God is our Hiding Place and you would like to show them what that means. Pick them up, carry them to a favorite spot, and sit there quietly, together. Remind them again that God will always be their Hiding Place, and he will keep them safe from trouble.

# CHAPTER 6

# God is Giver

## MEDITATE

*"Every good and perfect gift is from above, coming down from the Father of the heavenly lights, who does not change like shifting shadows."* – James 1:17 (NIV)

Extended passage: James 1:16-18

## ANTICIPATE

● What is the best gift you ever received? Who gave it to you?

_____

_____

● What gifts do you look forward to giving your child someday?

_____

_____

_____

I remember getting ready for my daughter Isabel's first Christmas. I made special presents for her and purchased special decorations for the tree. The energy and expectations for that first Christmas were sky high. I could not wait for Christmas to arrive. But once it did, I realized the first Christmas with a baby was pretty boring because our daughter had absolutely no idea what was going on. I was so excited and I wanted her to be excited too - to smile and pull the paper off each gift with flair and hug me for being so awesome and letting everyone she met that day know just how amazing this Christmas was (I told you the expectations were a little high).

## PRESCHOOL CHRISTMAS

Fast forward just a few years later. Christmas morning could not come soon enough for my kids. They wanted to extend the traditions and celebrate as much as possible. My daughters struggled to go to sleep but easily woke up at 4:00 a.m. and ran to our room to get the festivities started. Wrapping paper was ripped off the boxes with gusto and every gift was met with enthusiasm. There is a big difference between Christmas with a baby and Christmas with a preschooler. Not just in the excitement level for the celebration, but even in the gifts given.

## THE GIFT GIVER

In the book of James we learn God is an amazing gift giver. And the gifts we receive in this life - memorable moments, financial provision, meaningful friendships, grace and forgiveness, learning experiences, health and safety, even our children - they all come from God's hands. The beauty of this attribute of God is that God does not change. James makes that clear. God is always Giver. I have never reset the Christmas tree with another set of gifts on December 26th and 27th and 28th. But God never stops giving. We keep waking up each day to the goodness and gifts of our loving God.

Photo © AlohaHawaii

# BABY *Steps*

This week, take a walk with your child and while you are on the go, consider the gifts God has given you. Think beyond any physical things in your life and be sure to include relationships, memories, and more. List the gifts out and give thanks to God for providing these to you. Model this gratitude and appreciation with your baby in tow.

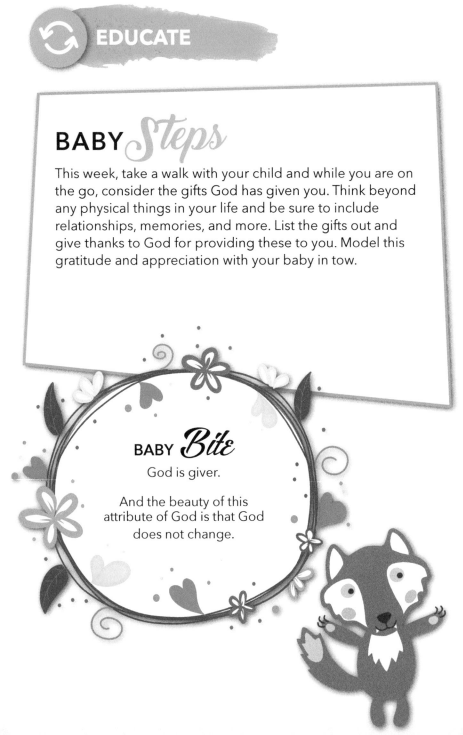

BABY *Bite*

God is giver.

And the beauty of this attribute of God is that God does not change.

## TODDLER *Tips*

God never stops giving.
We keep waking up each
day to the goodness and
gifts of our loving God.

# TODDLER *Steps*

Identify two or three gifts with your toddler that you can
give thanks to God for. Look around where you live,
search their room or go outside. If you can, keep the "gift"
in a prominent place. Be mindful of this gift throughout
the week and continue to appreciate God with your child.
As you acknowledge each gift, say "God, you give us
good and perfect gifts. Thank you for your amazing gift of
_____ this week."

# CHAPTER 7

# God is Father

## MEDITATE

*"At that time Jesus said, "I praise you, Father, Lord of heaven and earth, because you have hidden these things from the wise and learned, and revealed them to little children." – Matthew 11:25 (NIV)*

Extended passage: Matthew 11:25-30

## ANTICIPATE

● What were your first words?

_____

_____

● What were your child's first words?

_____

_____

_____

First words. It is amazing that as parents, we get to teach our children how to describe the world around them. As our children grow and learn words, they often repeat the sounds they hear. We all know a story of a child whose first word was a swear word. It happens. Now I must selfishly admit: I wanted the first word my children verbalized to be "dada." I tried everything possible to make them say this before anything else. I whispered "dada" in their ear, I repeated the word over and over again times 10,000, I put my child's hands on my mouth to feel the word as I said it, I moved my child's lips in the rhythm of the word...I tried all of these things because being a parent makes you crazy.

## VICTORY

So how did I do?

My children's first words were...1st child: **"Uh-oh"**, 2nd: **"More"**, 3rd: **"Bel-Bel"**, 4th: **"DADA"**! I can't be sure this is true, but I'm just going to declare victory and move on with life.

## ABBA

In Matthew 11, Jesus calls God "Father." The Hebrew word for "Father" is "Abba" which has been translated by Bible scholars as "Daddy." Jesus uses a personal, relational term to speak of God. This is a revolutionary concept because when you search the Old Testament, references to God as "Father" are scarce. God is referred to more as "Creator." But in the New Testament, all of that changes. Jesus refers to God as "Father" over 175 times, making "Father" the most common way Jesus talks about God. Guess what? You and I can refer to God in the same intimate way Jesus did. The Bible makes it clear: through Christ, we have access to God the Father. God is our Father. We are God's adopted children and adoption into God's family is not based on what we can do – he chose us before we could do anything to convince him otherwise. Understanding and celebrating this truth lies at the heart of our faith.

Photo © zulufoto

# BABY *Steps*

Babies experience a myriad of "firsts" before their first birthday, and as parents we love to celebrate these milestones. We take pictures of our child to show how they grow - next to blocks, signs, with special outfits indicating how many weeks and months old they are. We celebrate their first laugh, haircut, solid food, teeth, swim, Halloween, Thanksgiving, Christmas, crawl, birthday, selfie, snow (warmer climates excluded), and word. This is an important season to mark these milestones. Spiritually, we can celebrate who God is and what he has done with our babies and toddlers. So celebrate God as your heavenly Father. This week, pray God will reveal who he is to your baby. Pray that by God's grace, they will know - deeply and profoundly - the love he has for them as a Father.

## BABY *Bite*

The Hebrew word for "Father" is "Abba," which has been translated by Bible scholars as "Daddy." Jesus uses a personal, relational term to speak of God.

## TODDLER *Tips*

The amazing thing is that you and I can refer to God in the same intimate way Jesus did.

# TODDLER *Steps*

Toddlers continue to grow and experience exciting milestones. Language and vocabulary dramatically increases for toddlers around eighteen months and older. This is a wonderful time to help them say first words to God. Celebrate who God is and what he has done with your toddler. This week, invite them to pray with you and address God as "heavenly Father."

# CHAPTER 8

# God is Kind

## MEDITATE

*The LORD is tender and kind. He is gracious. He is slow to get angry. He is full of love.* – Psalm 103:8

Extended passage: Psalm 103

## ANTICIPATE

● What actions or situations typically trigger an angry response from you?

_____

_____

_____

● Who have you been quick to become angry with this week?

_____

_____

_____

Isabel was 13 and a half months old when her baby sister Sofia was born. I was equal parts nervous and excited when I introduced the two of them, both just babies that I hoped would become best friends. Isabel loved her sister fiercely from Day 1, but some days she was more fierce than loving.

## REACTING

I remember the first time she walked up to baby Sofi, sitting peacefully in her bouncer, and smacked her On. The. Head. Logically, I knew that Isabel wasn't capable of understanding how fragile her sister was, or that she had caused her pain. But instinctively, I was moved to protect one daughter while I was also shocked at the aggression from my other daughter. I reacted in anger. I picked Isabel up with hands that were not tender, I spoke to her in a tone that was not kind. There was no grace in my eyes as I commanded, "we do NOT hit!" I calmed Sofia and took some deep breaths.

## GOD-LIKE RESPONSE

Calmer now myself, I responded to Isabel as I should have from the beginning. Instead of being quick to anger, I was kind – reflective of the way God responds to me. Kindness here implies that our actions don't receive the response they deserve. Verse 10 goes on to say *"He doesn't pay us back in keeping with the evil things we've done."* This doesn't mean that God won't discipline us; Scripture is clear that God corrects our course when we wander off hIs path by choice or by mistake. But it speaks to his motivation – he corrects us because he is full of love for us. And out of that love, he treats us tenderly, with kindness that we don't deserve, offering grace we can't earn. When we reach out aggressively, when we provoke, he is slow to anger. Our little ones will test limits and try patience. It takes effort, trading in our knee-jerk reactions for Godlike responses. But in slowing our anger and responding in kindness instead of inkind, we point our child to their heavenly Father.

Photo © Olga Sapegina

# BABY *Steps*

While infants may not provoke our anger by being intentionally defiant or difficult, caring for a baby can be exhausting – physically, mentally, and emotionally. As a parent, you will at times experience frustration, feel overwhelmed, and find yourself at the end of your rope. Couple these things with a lack of sleep and pressure to succeed as a mom or dad, and you may find yourself becoming angry, and struggling to respond to your baby with tenderness, kindness, and grace. The next time you notice yourself becoming angry, consecrate that moment and your child to God. Speak a blessing over them by reading Psalm 103:8 aloud. Meditate on the verse throughout the week so that its words become familiar, and God's response begins to become your habit.

## BABY *Bite*

He corrects us because he is full of love for us. And out of that love, he treats us tenderly, with kindness that we don't deserve, offering grace we can't earn.

It takes effort, trading in our knee-jerk reactions for God-like responses. But in slowing our anger and responding in kindness instead of inkind, we point our child to their heavenly Father.

# TODDLER *Steps*

As your toddler begins to assert their independence, you may find yourself becoming angry in response. It helps me to remember that my child is not acting out against me – what may seem like defiance is often curiosity and a desire to gain some control over themselves and the situation at hand. This phase of testing boundaries is hard on everyone. Your toddler needs to learn limits and become independent, but the journey to becoming a big kid is messy and bumpy and everyone gets scraped up a bit on the way. When you notice your child reacting in anger, or when you find yourself becoming angry, consecrate that difficult moment by reading Psalm 103:8 as a blessing over your child. Invite your toddler to repeat some of the words after you – you could add in a melody and sing the song, or add in motions and act it out. Repeat this process throughout the week as the situation arises. Let the words become written on your heart and your child's, taking steps to respond more like God – with tender kindness, showing grace, slow to anger, full of love.

# CHAPTER 9

# God is the Light of the World

## 📖 MEDITATE

*When Jesus spoke again to the people, he said, "I am the light of the world. Whoever follows me will never walk in darkness, but will have the light of life."* – John 8:12 (NIV)

Extended passage: John 8:12-17

## ✏️ ANTICIPATE

- As a child, do you remember falling asleep on a long car ride home? Who brought you up to your room to go to sleep?

_____

_____

- Growing up, what feelings did you have about the dark?

_____

_____

_____

Growing up, my grandparents lived fifty miles away and my family would often take day trips to visit them in our blue Ford station wagon with faux wood paneling. My brother and I would sit in the "way back" and make funny faces at the cars we passed. After a long day with our grandparents, we would pile back into the station wagon and make the drive home. Because I never wore a seatbelt (I'm not sure the car even had them), I curled up on the floor and fell asleep. I have so many memories of my dad picking me up, carrying me to my room, and putting me in my bunk bed (complete with Smurf sheets because I was super rad). When I became a dad, I started making memories of getting our little ones out of the car after a tiring day, being extra careful not to wake them, walking as softly as possible to their cribs and laying them to rest after a long drive home from visiting my parents.

## LIGHT

Yet even if I handled my baby with the utmost care, made my way to their room like a ninja ballerina while holding my breath, placed them like a delicate flower in their bed but forgot to turn on their nightlight, they would wake up. Every time. The nightlight was the key to the whole process. I could not forget to turn on the night light. The type of night light did not matter. Maybe you're like me and you have purchased every nightlight imaginable. Character nightlight. LED night light. Soft nightlight. Princess castle nightlight. Sing and dance with me karaoke night light. Ok, that last one was made up. Somehow the light was a comfort in the dark, even to a sleeping baby.

In the book of John, Jesus refers to himself as the "light of the world." And when we follow in His footsteps, darkness will never shade our path. Darkness simply hides from the light of God before us. And in this light, we are comforted and we need not fear for we know our God has brought us life.

Photo © Hannamariah

47

# BABY *Steps*

Babies often struggle with learning to fall asleep and stay asleep. Often times, they fall asleep in our arms, and as soon as we put them down, they awaken and want to be held. Learning to sleep is hard work for a baby and takes time, but you can begin teaching them that Jesus is always with them, even in the darkness of night. As you carry your sleeping baby from your car or couch to their crib and turn on their nightlight, say "Jesus tells us he is the Light of the World."

## BABY *Bite*

Jesus refers to himself as the "light of the world." And when we follow in his footsteps, darkness will never shade our path.

## TODDLER *Tips*

Darkness simply hides from the light of God before us. And in this light, we are comforted and we need not fear for we know our God has brought us life.

# TODDLER *Steps*

Toddlers are more apt to be afraid of the dark. They are curious and imaginative and struggle to distinguish what is real from what is pretend. A toddler's overactive imagination tends to kick into high gear once they are tucked in to bed, where it is quiet and dark. Help them address this by letting them turn off the light in their room. Encourage them to flip the switch a couple of times, so they can see the light and dark. As they turn off the light, share John 8:12.

# CHAPTER 10

# God is the Morning Star

## 📖 MEDITATE

*We couldn't be more sure of what we saw and heard – God's glory, God's voice. The prophetic Word was confirmed to us. You'll do well to keep focusing on it. It's the one light you have in a dark time as you wait for daybreak and the rising of the Morning Star in your hearts.*

– 2 Peter 1:19 (MSG)

Extended passage: 2 Peter 1:12-21

## ✏️ ANTICIPATE

● What circumstances have made you feel hopeless recently?

_____

_____

_____

● Where do you most need a light at the end of the tunnel?

_____

_____

_____

While there are only 13½ months between my first and second born girls, there is a seven year gap between my girls and my son Zion. While I planned some space between my second and third babies, I didn't plan on struggling through infertility and a miscarriage, followed by a difficult pregnancy. Time seemed to stand still in those hard months.

## LIGHT AT THE END

When Zion finally arrived, I vowed to treasure every moment with him and he made that vow easy to keep. Some of that was his temperament, but some of that was mine as well. Where I was unsure of myself with my first two babies, I was confident and calm with my third. I understood how quickly those sleepless nights would pass, and how soon those days spent rocking, feeding, and carrying a baby on my hip would be over. So in the midst of a difficult phase, I could see the light at the end of the tunnel. Or as Peter may have described it, I knew the sun was rising because I could see the Morning Star – the star that rises just before dawn – bringing hope in the midst of darkness.

## FOCUS ON CHRIST

Peter's tone as he opens his letter is urgent as he urges the church to focus on Jesus. Maybe they felt overwhelmed or they struggled to find hope in the midst of their troubles. Have you ever found yourself waiting for daybreak? Whether it's a sleepless night that just won't end, or a painful struggle that won't loosen its grip, dark times make us desperate for light. But the Good News for us is that the Light is already here. In the darkness, in the waiting for daybreak, the Morning Star rises in our hearts. *We just need to know where to look.* Peter once failed to see the light at the end of the tunnel, and he felt the regret of giving up hope. His words are a gift that can keep us from making his mistake. We don't have to cower in darkness; we can stand boldly, waiting for daybreak, our Savior risen and living in our hearts.

Photo © aporokh at gmail dot com

# BABY *Steps*

Babies love to look at the contrast of black against white. As a newborn, when their eyesight is still developing, those sharp contrasts are easier to focus on. Draw a white star on a black sheet of paper (or if you're more crafty and talented than I am, feel free to create something more Pinterest-worthy) and place it somewhere in your baby's room as a reminder that God brings hope in the darkness – He is the Morning Star that rises just before dawn. Show it to your baby often, giving them time to focus their eyes on the picture as you focus your heart on God.

### BABY *Bite*

But the Good News for us is that the Light is already here.

We don't have to cower in darkness, feeling abandoned by a Savior led to die. We can stand boldly, waiting for daybreak, our Savior risen and living in our hearts.

# TODDLER *Steps*

Toddlers are beginning to name objects and can recognize them at a distance. Take your toddler out one night to see the stars – point to them and tell them that they give us light when it's dark. Then have them "draw" their own stars – have them use white fingerpaint or a crayon to draw on a dark sheet of paper. Read 2 Peter 1:19 and share that just like God gives us light when the sky gets dark, he also gives us hope when things are hard. While they may not fully understand the concept, God promises that his Word will never return void, and giving them language for difficult concepts now will lay important groundwork for their comprehension later. Say a short prayer, thanking God for the stars in the sky and for sending Jesus to bring us hope.

# CHAPTER 11

# God is Our Peace

## MEDITATE

*Christ himself is our peace. He has made Jews and Gentiles into one group of people. He has destroyed the hatred that was like a wall between us.* – Ephesians 2:14

Extended passage: Ephesians 2:11-22

## ANTICIPATE

● What kind of parent would you categorize yourself as?

_____

_____

_____

● Who have you judged lately, simply because they were different than you?

_____

_____

## ♥ RELATE

Before having kids, I thought there were two clubs – Moms and Not Moms. Being a Not Mom, I figured all Moms generally were the same and moved around like a homogenized carpooling, PB&J making group, who chatted on playgrounds during playdates. Imagine my shock when I joined the Moms Club and realized that there were, in fact, many factions. Being a part-time work-from-home mom, I found myself wandering between the Working Mom and Stay at Home Mom camps, without being able to join either. Sometimes I felt judged and I'm embarrassed to admit that sometimes I was the one who passed judgment on another mom different from me.

## PARENTING TOGETHER

Then we became a Host Home with Safe Families for Children. As we provided shelter for children whose parents were in crisis, I parented alongside moms whose shoes had walked a harder road than mine. My preconceived notions on poverty were called into question, and the wall separating Me and Them came tumbling down as I sat down next to brave women who laid awake all night, protecting their babies in homeless shelters, or who packed up their entire lives into a backpack.

## TEARING DOWN WALLS

I learned that it's easy to judge someone when I saw them as different. But when Jesus steps in the middle and calls me to connect with someone, he breaks down walls. Our world is filled with discord and judgment, and on our own we are likely to build walls with hatred we don't even recognize until it's too late.

We separate ourselves into Us and Them. But Jesus came to be Peace. He calls us his children, adopts us into his family, and isn't interested in factions or subgroups. As parents, we have the opportunity to invite peace into our home and raise our children to build a world without walls. But first we have to recognize the walls we have built, and invite Christ to remove them.

Photo © Tatyana Vyc

55

# BABY *Steps*

Babies are learning to make sense of the world around them, and they pick up subtle cues from the environments they are exposed to. If they are only exposed to people who are "like" them in race, culture, abilities, etc, they will naturally learn to exclude those who are different from them. You can help them build diverse relationships by exposing them to diverse environments. Bring them to a park in a different neighborhood, or a festival that celebrates another culture. Befriend families who have children with special needs, or who speak a different language. Within your faith community, look for mentors who are farther along in their journey, and mentor others who come behind. As you encounter barriers that separate you or your child from others, pray God's Peace will destroy those walls.

### BABY *Bite*

When Jesus steps in the middle and calls me to connect with someone, he breaks down walls and plows common ground.

## TODDLER *Tips*

As parents, we have the opportunity to invite Peace into our home and raise our children to build a world without walls.

# TODDLER *Steps*

Toddlers continue to make sense of the world around them and are beginning to develop language to communicate with and befriend others. In another year or two, they will have developed preferences for people who are "like" them and those they are most familiar with, and may be fearful of those who seem "different." Continue building diverse relationships, and discuss differences as they arise. Reading books together about people with diverse backgrounds and abilities will help provide language for discussing those differences. Be sensitive to situations where your toddler feels uncomfortable around someone who may seem "different," and pray with and for them, that God would be the Peace that breaks through any walls that would come between them.

# CHAPTER 12

# God is Quieter

## MEDITATE

*The LORD your God is with you. He is the Mighty Warrior who saves. He will take great delight in you. In his love he will no longer punish you. Instead, he will sing for joy because of you.* – Zephaniah 3:17

Extended passage: Zephaniah 3

## ANTICIPATE

● How often do you experience quiet in your day?

_____

_____


● What do you enjoy doing when it is quiet??

_____

_____

_____

## ♥ RELATE

With each of my children, I chose a verse for them while I was still pregnant. I came across this verse in Zephaniah when I was pregnant with Zion; it stuck out to me because the previous verse prefaces by saying "Zion, don't be afraid. Don't give up." I chose this verse for him both because of its message, and because it calls him by name. God is speaking to his children here, warning them of judgment. He reminds me of a father, broken-hearted as he disciplines a wayward child for his own good: "And I would not have had to punish you so much. But you still wanted to go on sinning in every way you could." (v7) His words of warning turn to a promise of restoration, as he looks forward to the day when his children will correct their course and turn to him so they can begin again.

## DISCIPLINE

When we hold our newborns, helpless and dependant on us to survive, it's hard to imagine the day when we will have to discipline them. But babies grow quickly into toddlers, and the work of guiding them on the right path begins. The first few times I disciplined Zion were painful for both of us. He is still my child that crumbles at correction, and I have to be very careful as I choose my words and tone so that he recognizes his mistake as an action and not his identity.

## RESTORATION

While discipline is painful, restoration is comforting. As an adult, I often experience discipline in the form of natural consequences. Sometimes I beat myself up over poor choices, but God offers me the hope of restoration. He promises that the quietness of his love will calm me down. I don't know about you, but I don't experience a lot of quiet moments as a mom. Quietness is something I savor. I love the thought of God's love as quietness – a calm moving into my storm. This week, when you are confronted with the consequences of your own sin, take time to allow the quietness of his love to calm you down.

# BABY *Steps*

While infants are too young to learn from discipline, they can certainly experience quiet as calming. Create a quiet place or routine that will calm your baby when they become upset. It could be a rocking chair in a corner of their room, or a soft blanket wrapped around them, or a lullaby sung quietly as you sway back and forth. Make a habit of using this place or routine when your baby is upset. Let your child know that you love them and that God loves them, too.

## BABY *Bite*

When we hold our newborns, helpless and dependant on us to survive, it's hard to imagine the day when we will have to discipline them. But babies grow quickly into toddlers, and the work of guiding them on the right path begins.

## TODDLER *Tips*

While discipline
is painful, restoration
is comforting.

## TODDLER *Steps*

As your toddler begins to explore and test limits, they
sometimes need redirection. At times, this will include
discipline - training or correction that shows them the
right path. Create a quiet place or routine that will calm
your toddler and offer restoration after you correct or
discipline them. It could be a moment in their room where
you give a hug and encouraging words, or a time spent
rocking your child in their favorite chair while reminding
them that they are loved. You may want to have your
toddler help choose a "Quiet Place" and stock it with a
favorite toy or blanket. Visit this place when your child
needs to calm down, and create a routine of returning
with your child to this place whenever they need a
moment of restoration. Remind them that you love and
take joy in them, and that God does, too.

# CHAPTER 13

# *God is Strength*

## MEDITATE

*For the director of music. Of David the servant of the LORD. He sang to the LORD the words of this song when the LORD delivered him from the hand of all his enemies and from the hand of Saul. He said: I love you, LORD, my strength.* – Psalm 18:1 (NIV)

Extended passage: Psalm 18:1-50

## ANTICIPATE

● Have you ever participated in athletic training of any kind (sport, race, fitness)?

_____

_____

_____

● What did you do to get stronger?

_____

_____

When I was 16, I sped down a side street to get to work faster and completely blew a stop sign. The car I was driving and the car I hit were completely totalled. I remember shaking uncontrollably, completely in shock and afraid of the trouble I would be in. Because this car crash happened before the era of smartphones and OnStar, I have no idea how my parents found out I was in an accident. Eventually my dad drove to the crash scene and walked right up to me outside the ambulance. My dad came so close – his face was only two inches away from my own – and he hugged me. No words. And I will never forget it.

## HANDS

Years later as I became a dad and I held each one of my young children in my arms, I became struck by their sheer smallness. Their little baby hands and baby feet – everything so incredibly tiny! And while a baby's hands are clenched for the first four months, one of the things I loved to do was put my finger in their hand. I was often surprised at how strong their grip was. And with my finger wrapped up in my infant's tiny hand, I was filled with love. Every time.

## STRENGTH

We already covered the story of David escaping King Saul's deathly pursuit in chapter 4. Here in Psalm 18, we read a similar version of the song of David in 2 Samuel 22. One of the differences between these parallel passages is verse 1. David declares his love for the Lord and then refers to the Lord as "my strength." David recognizes God was the only reason he was sustained through Saul's attempts to put him to death. David did not end up in the hand of his enemies or in Saul's hand because David was in God's strong, mighty hand. Somehow love and strength are inexorably tied together here in David's song of praise. Just like the moment between me and my dad at the crash site and my young children squeezing my finger in their hand.

Photo © Gino Santa Maria

63

# BABY *Steps*

We communicate unparalleled love for our children when we hold them. Every one of their senses is engaged as they are held close in our arms, and they find safety and comfort there. They feel our touch, hear our heartbeat, and mirror our eye contact. As parents, may we never stop holding our children. This week, hold and squeeze your infant tight. Give them extra snuggles. Rock them just a moment longer. Put aside any distractions that might keep you from being fully present. As you give them a squeeze, remind them that God is their strength.

## BABY *Bite*

David did not end up in the hand of his enemies or in Saul's hand because David was in God's strong, mighty hand.

## TODDLER

Love and strength are
inexorably tied together
here in David's song
of praise.

# TODDLER *Steps*

During the toddler years, we communicate a great deal
with them through our body language. They learn from
our eyes, posture, and facial expressions in addition to
our words. Toddlers understand and respond to the
emotion behind eye contact and physical touch. As
adults, we often give more thought to our words than
our nonverbal signals, but your toddler studies those
signals and even begins to mirror them. They learn to
hug, because we hug them. They learn to shake their
head and say "no" because we have modeled it for
them. It's important to be intentional with your body
language. Throughout the week, get on your toddler's
level and look them eye to eye. Give them big bear
hugs. Teach them to hug you back as tight as they can –
until they collapse! Trade bear hugs and talk about the
strength needed to give a big hug. Remind your child
that God is strong and loving.

# Creation – a Beginning

## 📖 MEDITATE

*"In the beginning, God created the heavens and the earth."*
– Genesis 1:1

Extended passage: Genesis 1:1-2:2

## ✏️ ANTICIPATE

● What do you recall about the evening of your baby's Birth Day?

_____

_____

_____

● What emotions did you experience? What surprised you?

_____

_____

_____

I remember the evening of each of my babies' Birth Days. After the excitement of labor and delivery had passed, the guests had left, and the first feedings and baths had been completed, the nurses turned down the lights and it was finally just us. It was always an ethereal moment as I held this new little one who felt so much a part of me and yet so much a stranger. I had sensed them move and grow inside of me and yet now I wondered who they would grow to be. I studied their features - a button nose or curly locks or blue eyes. This moment always felt like the real beginning for me. This moment was always when I was struck with the wonder that I was their mom.

## THE BEGINNING

Genesis tells us about another beginning. We know only one thing about what was before this beginning - "In the beginning, God." Before creation, before The Beginning, there was God. In times where my world seems thrown off its orbit, I find comfort in knowing that God always Was and always Will Be. Out of eternity, God spoke and the world began. The narrative goes on to describe all that God created - everything around us, the sights and sounds and smells that make this world our home, he literally spoke into existence.

## GOD IS PRESENT

Scripture reveals a God that knows everything, is everywhere, and exists outside the boundaries of time and space. This moment that you are in, he knew about it before the world began. The life you live and the people you love are part of the story he wrote before you took your first breath. He has prepared you for this moment. He will prepare you for the moments to come. The same voice that spoke and light appeared, speaks to you now. The power that unfurled ocean tides, carries you now. So if you stand at the beginning of a journey, know that the God who was already present at the first Beginning, is present in this beginning, and all that will follow.

Photo © Syda Productions

# BABY *Steps*

Take time this week with your baby to look through photos of their Birth Day. Talk about the moments that stand out in your memory – share what it was like to see their face for the first time, to hear their cry, to hold them in your arms. Later, look back at the days before your baby's birth. Reflect on how your life has changed. Many parents experience a longing for their previous life, even though they love their baby. It's important to be honest with yourself and others about the range of feelings you experience. Left unchecked, these feelings can become overwhelming and distort the way you see yourself and the world around you. We all need someone to come alongside us on this journey, as a fellow traveler and as another guide for our child. This week, pray about who that someone could be. Then take an action step – call or message a friend and plan a time where you can reflect on the new beginnings in your life. Bring your baby along – it's never too early to introduce your little one to friends who will come alongside as fellow guides on the journey.

## BABY *Bite*

In times where my world seems thrown off its orbit, I find comfort in knowing that God always Was and always Will Be.

## TODDLER *Tips*

He has prepared you for this moment. He will prepare you for the moments to come.

# TODDLER *Steps*

Toddlers are beginning to identify themselves as "big kids" and are often fascinated with babies. Together, look through your child's baby photos and talk with them about how they've grown. Show them photos of their Birth Day, and share some favorite memories from that day. If friends or family visited in those early days, talk about them with your toddler, sharing with them how they are loved by you and by others. Invite one of those friends or family members over or plan a video call and have them share their thoughts or memories of your baby's Birth Day. Thank them for coming alongside you and helping you guide your child along the way. If you struggle to think of someone, pray that God will identify that person who would join you on your journey, as a support for you and as an example and guide for your child. Then take an action step and ask that person to join you and your child for an outing or playdate. Your toddler will benefit from another role model and you will be encouraged by a friend.

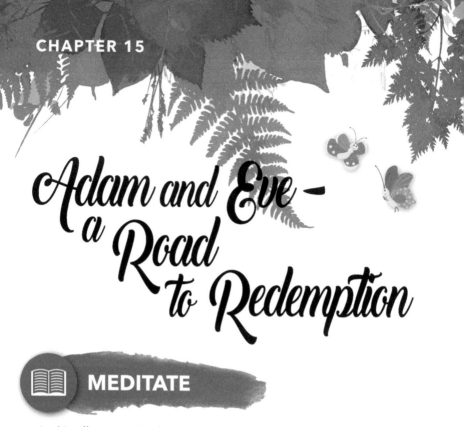

# CHAPTER 15

# Adam and Eve – a Road to Redemption

## MEDITATE

*And I will put enmity between you and the woman, and between your offspring and hers; he will crush your head, and you will strike his heel.*

– Genesis 3:15 (NIV)

Extended passage: Genesis 3:1-24

## ANTICIPATE

● What do you imagine the Garden of Eden looked like?

_____

_____

_____

● Do you remember a choice you made as a child that ended badly?

_____

_____

_____

"All gone." I said these words to my mom as I dropped an empty bottle of Tylenol on our apartment floor having just ingested an entire bottle the painkillers. My tiny toddler body managed to climb on top of the counter, get inside the kitchen cabinet, open the bottle and swallow every last pill. I ate what I wasn't supposed to and suddenly my life was in danger. My parents rushed me to the hospital to remedy the situation. Trust me, we do not need to go over how the emergency room handles this kind of thing. Can you imagine this happening in your house?

## ADAM AND EVE

Adam and Eve, fresh from Creation and all the majesty and perfection therein, ate something they shouldn't have. Adam and Eve did not misconstrue God's instructions – he was quite clear. God declared, "Do not eat the fruit from the tree of the knowledge of good and evil." They did it anyway. Adam and Eve only had one job to do and it was a complete failure. And after Adam and Eve sinned, God reveals a plan to bring back beauty from destruction. Right from the beginning of The Story, redemption is found in the pages of God's book.

## PLANS

The story of Jesus redeeming us from sin and death is the greatest story and we have an opportunity to share it with our children. We can be the ones to tell them about Adam and Eve, their choice to disobey God, and God's response. But it will take a plan to make it happen. As parents, we love plans, right? We will make plans for our kid's sleep schedule. We will make plans for home improvement. We will make detailed plans for holiday celebrations – first birthdays, Christmas, or 4th of July. We will schedule our work day in 30 minute blocks, yet creating a plan for sharing God's Story with our children can fall by the wayside.

# BABY *Steps*

God made a redemption plan and you have the privilege of introducing your child to that plan. This week, read the Bible to your baby. Open up a storybook Bible and read the story of Adam and Eve. Say, "God gives us Jesus to redeem us – to take away our bad choices and help us know God."

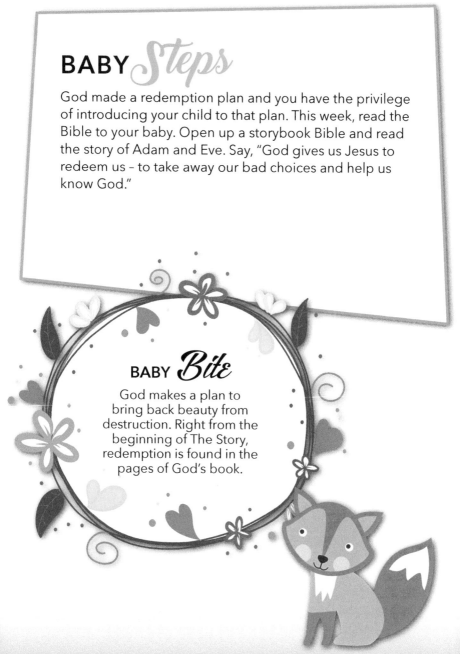

## BABY *Bite*

God makes a plan to bring back beauty from destruction. Right from the beginning of The Story, redemption is found in the pages of God's book.

## TODDLER *Tips*

The story of Jesus redeeming us from sin and death is the greatest story and we have an opportunity to share it with our children.

# TODDLER *Steps*

The toddler years involve learning to make choices. Toddlers learn to exert their will on the world around them. The word "No" is introduced to their vocabulary. This week, give your toddler the opportunity to make lots of choices. As they make choices, talk about Adam and Eve eating the fruit. Remember, God's response to the bad choice was giving us Jesus.

# CHAPTER 16

# Noah – He Rescues

## MEDITATE

*The LORD then said to Noah, "Go into the ark, you and your whole family, because I have found you righteous in this generation.*

– Genesis 7:1 (NIV)

Extended passage: Genesis 7:1-24

## ANTICIPATE

● Have you ever experienced being rescued? What happened?

_____

_____

_____

● How have you rescued your child from a difficult or dangerous situation?

_____

_____

_____

Who would have thought a splash pad would be the place I totally scared someone else's toddler? *On purpose.* Let me explain. We took our toddler to the local splash pad, found a spot next to the sand and water tables and watched her go to work. Toddlers can become very serious about their play and Isabel was no exception. She was crafting a messy masterpiece, but a little boy kept pestering her. Little pushes. Grabbing her shovel. Flinging sand.

## CHOICES

I tried to give the other child the benefit of the doubt. "Isabel, your friend really likes sand doesn't he? Why don't you come play on this side so he can have more to build his castle?" That did not work so I tried another tactic. "Isabel, I think you should play over here where you won't have to worry about getting in anyone's way." The young boy was persistent. But when he filled a shovel with wet sand and walked up to my daughter and flung it in directly in her face, I stood up and grabbed the shovel from his hand and tossed it aside. The little boy ran away. My daughter ran to me. To this day, she remembers the day I rescued her from the "mean boy."

## RESCUE

Genesis 6 reveals a world gone bad and highlights a dramatic difference in God's response to his creation. In Genesis 1:31, God identifies creation as "very good" and in Genesis 6:6, "The Lord regretted that he had made human beings on the earth, and his heart was deeply troubled." So God's plan was simple: start again. But in the middle of all the mess, God noticed Noah and his family. Noah was a righteous man and God rescued Noah and his family from the ensuing flood using an ark. The ark God asked Noah to build was an immense ship measuring 450 feet long, 75 feet wide, and 45 feet high. After the flood waters receded, God made a covenant with Noah never to flood the earth again. Noah's story reveals the God who rescues. He doesn't leave us in the mess we created, he saves us from it.

Photo © Philippe Put

# BABY *Steps*

Babies are unable to protect themselves from danger, and rely on their parents to keep them safe. They often do surprising things that you do not expect or anticipate – wriggle toward the edge of a bouncer, crawl toward the end of your bed, eat things off the floor that will make them sick. They are just gaining control of their bodies, and they don't know how to use that control to stay safe. How can a parent model rescue for their baby? Pick them up when they cry or get hurt. Use the word "rescue" as you lift them up and give them a squeeze. Remind them of a time you knew God's rescue in your own life.

## BABY *Bite*

Noah's story reveals the God who rescues. He doesn't leave us in the mess we created, he saves us from it.

## TODDLER *Tips*

God's plan was simple: start again. But in the middle of all the mess, God noticed Noah and his family.

# TODDLER *Steps*

Toddlers are eager to explore and try out their newfound mobility. They keep you on your toes, always climbing and maneuvering and often falling. How can a parent model rescue for their toddler? When your toddler is walking and about to trip, your first inclination may be to never let them fall. It's okay for kids to fall down (don't we want them to learn to get back up?). We want our kids not just to learn to fall down or to get back up, but to know that God finds them in the places where they are in need. God's rescue will always be there for them.

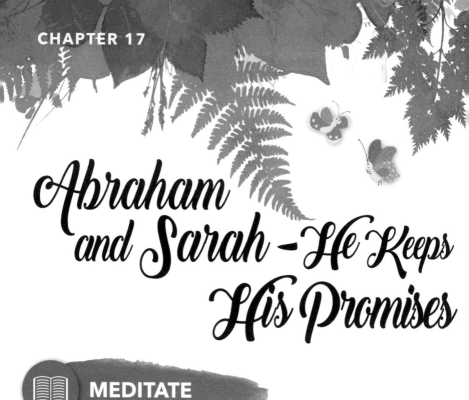

# CHAPTER 17

# Abraham and Sarah – He Keeps His Promises

## 📖 MEDITATE

*I will make my covenant with you last forever. It will be between me and you and your family after you for all time to come. I will be your God. And I will be the God of all your family after you." – Genesis 17:7*

Extended passage: Genesis 17:1-9

## ✏️ ANTICIPATE

● What are all of the ways you've met your child's needs in the past 24 hours?

_____

_____

_____

● How did your child communicate those needs?

_____

_____

I remember the first few times I had to leave my baby with another caregiver. Suddenly I had to communicate everything my baby needed and how I met that need in simple, easy to remember instructions. I could quickly jot down a basic schedule, but there were so many aspects of their care that were more nuanced. I walked away, thinking of how I'd left my baby helpless and dependent on someone who couldn't know them the way I did. I was their mom, and I was torn between the need to be with my child and the need to be away from them.

## A FAITHFUL GOD

In Genesis 17, God reestablishes his covenant with Abraham (because Abraham had tried to take matters into his own hands when he doubted God's first covenant). But God reveals himself to be faithful, even when we are faithless. He makes a promise between himself and Abraham...*and the children not yet born to him.* God knew what his children needed – they needed a God who would be with them. A God who would be faithful in the midst of their faithlessness. And while this established covenant required obedience, God foresaw their disobedience and would send his Son to fulfill the covenant when they failed to hold up their end of the bargain. Even in the midst of our failure, God steps in and meets our need with a Savior.

## GOD WITH US

While we learn our baby's needs and how to meet them through trial and error, God knows exactly what we need and how to provide for us before we can even ask. And he never steps away from us. Not for a moment. He is not torn between *with us* and *away from us.* This is his promise to us. This is his promise to our children. While God established his covenant with Abraham, and called that he respond with obedience, we know that Jesus fulfilled the covenant and our response should be to put our faith and trust in him. By believing in Jesus and allowing him to guide us along the journey, we receive the full benefits of God's covenant.

Photo © Tatyana Vyc

# BABY

While an infant is too young to make a commitment to follow Christ, God has given us the responsibility of passing on our faith by studying his Word and teaching it to our children (Deuteronomy 11:18-20). By reading this devotional, you're already on the right path! Take time to dedicate your baby. Make a formal commitment to pass on your faith and entrust your child in his hands, knowing that he has promised to be their God. It could be as simple as writing a promise and adding your signature and date. Or you could inquire about your church's child dedication service. Then get started (or continue on!). Take time to read God's Word each day, pray with and for your child, and create a rhythm where you speak about God and his Word as you go about your day. Scripture spoken at wake up time, prayers at mealtime, bedtime blessings – these are simple ways to point your child to God.

## BABY

God knew what his children needed – they needed a God who would be with them. A God who would be faithful in the midst of their faithlessness.

TODDLER *Tips*

By believing in Jesus and
allowing him to guide
us along the journey, we
receive the full benefits of
God's covenant.

# TODDLER *Steps*

Your toddler is likely still too young to make a commitment to follow Christ, but as they are developing language, it is a great time to start sharing more of your faith with them. If you haven't already, dedicate your child. If you've already dedicated your child, tell your toddler about it and remind them often: "I've dedicated you to God. I trust that He will take care of you and I promise to teach you about him." Talk about God throughout the day - tell your toddler that God made the grass at their favorite park, thank God for making the food they're about to eat, remind them at bedtime that God promises to be with them always. Give your child easy to understand reminders like these that the God you love is their God, too.

# CHAPTER 18

# Joseph – Evil Turns to Good

## 📖 MEDITATE

*But Joseph said to them, "Don't be afraid. Am I in the place of God? You intended to harm me, but God intended it for good to accomplish what is now being done, the saving of many lives.* – Genesis 50:19-20 (NIV)

Extended passage: Genesis 50:15-21

## ✏️ ANTICIPATE

● When you think about your family's future. What does it look like?

_____

_____

● What's on your five-year plan?

_____

_____

I remember finishing college and making my five-year plan. It was an amazing plan - filled with optimism, brimming with possibility. I identified where I would work, scheduled how our family would grow, budgeted for when we would buy a starter home and move into our forever home. It was a perfect plan.

## SURPRISE

Looking back, my life did not always go as planned. In fact, most of the time my life veered off the plan.

**Where I would work** - After college, instead of moving to a new city and starting new jobs we moved back to our hometown. I applied three times to my dream workplace and was rejected three times. **When our family would grow** - Instead of having kids every two years, our first two children were 13 months apart - and our third 7 years later. More than once along the way, we faced the heartache of hearing the words, "You've lost the pregnancy." **When we would buy a house** - The house we bought as a starter home, we still own.

## JOSEPH

Beginning in Genesis 37 we read about a boy named Joseph. He is probably most famous for being the favored son of Jacob who receives a multi-colored coat. But Joseph's story begins with the dreams he has that make his brothers angry. As a young man, I am certain Joseph's five-year plan did not include all God ended up leading him through.

Joseph endures: being sold into slavery, going to prison for a crime he did not commit, becoming the second most powerful person in Egypt, reuniting with his family after years of estrangement, and establishing God's people in Egypt. When our plans are undone, what God is trying to accomplish in our lives is unleashed. What Joseph's brothers meant for evil God used for good.

Photo © Ana Blazic Pavlovic

# BABY

From the moment you knew you were having a baby, you have probably been dreaming about their future. It is good to make plans, and to put your dreams on paper. But before you lock into the 5-year plan, submit it to God. Hold the plan loosely because God just might have something more. This week, dream about and for your baby. What dreams do you have for their lives? Listen to the Holy Spirit – is there something you sense God might do in your child's life? Write it all down. Mark the plan with a handprint or footprint. Don't forget to include your own. Talk about the dreams and plans God inspires in you with your infant. Ask questions and wonder together about what God has in store.

BABY *Bite*

God's plan for Joseph was
not what he expected,
it was better.

## TODDLER *Tips*

When our plans are
undone, what God is trying
to accomplish in our lives
is unleashed.

# TODDLER *Steps*

Toddlers are just beginning to understand concepts of present, past, and future, and they enjoy routines and the predictability of following a plan. As toddlers grow into the preschool years, they learn to follow a daily plan. Routines and schedules are helpful tools to create stability in a toddler's life. This week create a fun, daily plan on paper. Think through your days together and come up with different blocks of time and activities (Reading Time, Outside Time, Quiet Play Time, Block Time, Bible Time, Doll Time, Lunch Time, etc…). As you go through the plan, inevitably you will change course. Let your toddler know it's okay when plans change. Remind them that we submit our plans to God, trusting that his plan is always the best plan.

# CHAPTER 19

# Moses – He Will Deliver

## 📖 MEDITATE

*So tell the people of Israel, "I am the LORD. I will throw off the heavy load the Egyptians have put on your shoulders. I will set you free from being slaves to them. I will reach out my arm and save you with mighty acts when I judge Egypt." – Exodus 6:6*

Extended passage: Exodus 6:1-12

## ✏️ ANTICIPATE

● Have you ever had to "rescue" your child from a predicament?

_____

_____

_____

● What struggle or burden do you need deliverance from?

_____

_____

I remember the first time I woke to hear my baby screaming. I heard fear and pain in her voice and I ran to her room. Protruding from her crib, stuck between the slats, was her chubby little arm. I wanted to pick her up as quickly as I could, but I had to carefully twist her arm to get it free. I checked her for injuries, but as soon as I scooped her up in my arms, she began to settle. Tears stopped, breathing slowed, and as it turned out, she wasn't really hurt. She had been trapped, and it probably was painful, but all she needed was for me to reach out to set her free.

## HOPELESS

The Israelites were in a different predicament, but were nonetheless trapped. They yearned for freedom but were held down by the Egyptians. So they cried out in the darkness for the God who felt far away to rescue them. What they didn't know is that God had a rescue plan already in the works. God sent Moses to share the good news but they didn't listen to him. They were hopeless and weary and because the situation felt impossible, they couldn't imagine that even God was capable of setting them free. Not unlike my daughter, pinned down in her crib, the Israelites were trapped. And the more they struggled, the more they felt the pain of their predicament. They cried out but couldn't fathom freedom, even when they heard it coming.

## DELIVERED

Sometimes we find ourselves in the same boat. We cry out to God for deliverance when the bills pile up or the relationship fractures or the plates we are spinning begin to drop. We know God's promise but we have lost hope and are buried under the work and freedom seems beyond our grasp. Moses reminds us that when hope is lost, God doesn't give up on us. Things may be bad, and they may even get worse, but nothing can stop the mighty hand of God. Cry out in the darkness and know that God hears, and that he is faithful to deliver us.

Photo © Dora Zett

# BABY *Steps*

In your baby's first year, they will learn countless new skills as they move from helpless newborn to walking toddler. You can help them practice these skills by giving them developmentally appropriate challenges. Give your newborn tummy time to help them develop stronger neck muscles and head control. Place a toy just out of your infant's reach to encourage rolling over or crawling. Hold onto your mobile infant's hand as they stand to help them take steps and develop those leg muscles. Working on these skills is important, but it is also hard work for your little one. When they become tired or overwhelmed, they may get "stuck" and will likely cry out for help. Let them know with words and actions that you are there to help. As you scoop them up or set them free, remind them that God is their deliverer.

## BABY *Bite*

They cried out of the darkness for the God who felt far away to come near and rescue them. What they didn't know is that God had a rescue plan already in the works.

## TODDLER *Tips*

Moses reminds us that when hope is lost, God doesn't give up on us. Things may be bad, and they may even get worse, but nothing can stop the mighty hand of God.

# TODDLER *Steps*

Toddlers continue to develop their walking, running, and climbing skills and are fine-tuning their coordination while also growing stronger. Choose a skill that your toddler needs more practice on and make a game out of working on that skill. Have them toss socks into a laundry basket, walk up stairs one foot after the next (instead of stepping on a stair with both feet), carry blocks across a room, etc. Once your child completes the task, add in another element of difficulty – move the laundry basket, "race" them up the stairs, give them more blocks, etc. As the task becomes more difficult, they may become frustrated or even angry and ask for help. Let them know you are there to help them and work on the task together. As you do so, remind them that God is their deliverer, or helper.

# CHAPTER 20

# David – You are His Masterpiece

## 📖 MEDITATE

*Jesse had seven of his sons walk in front of Samuel. But Samuel said to him, "The LORD hasn't chosen any of them." So he asked Jesse, "Are these the only sons you have?" "No," Jesse answered. "My youngest son is taking care of the sheep." – I Samuel 16:10-11*

Extended passage: 1 Samuel 16:1-13

## ✏️ ANTICIPATE

● What is your favorite thing about your child?

_____

_____

_____

● Which of your child's traits or habits cause frustration?

_____

_____

_____

When my daughter Isabel was just under a year old, she looked at me mid-meltdown and slapped me. In. The. Face. I remember seeking out advice in the months that followed on how to "deal with" a strong-willed child and I came across an exercise that had me chart my daughter's "difficult" behaviors, along with the corresponding "positive" behaviors. So while her stubbornness exasperated me, her determination was admirable. Her heightened emotions were the flipside of a tender and compassionate heart.

## PERSPECTIVE

It was a simple exercise, but it convicted me that my role as parent wasn't to "change" my child, either by controlling her problematic behaviors or rewarding more admirable ones. My role was to come alongside the Holy Spirit. God knit her together in my womb, he already knows the masterpiece she will become, and I get a front row seat to her unveiling. It takes some of the pressure off, yes. But it also challenges me to be more observant, as every brush stroke reveals a key to the greater design.

## THE SHEPHERD

I wonder if Jesse had one of those "aha" moments after his youngest son David was chosen to be the next king. David was trained as a shepherd. A seemingly meaningless detail at the time, but the significance of David the shepherd would unfold throughout God's Story. It was his experience as a shepherd, fighting beasts in the field with God's help that would give him confidence to defeat Goliath. David's days herding sheep would give voice to Psalm 23, where he paints a picture of God as our shepherd. And someday Jesus himself, a Son of David, would proclaim himself the Great Shepherd. Thankfully, God uses our parenting skills (or lack thereof). We have the honor of preparing our children to do the work that God has already begun in them. Their uniqueness is all part of the masterpiece God will reveal in them over time.

Photo © Karve

# BABY *Steps*

Even young babies begin to show signs of their temperament and personality. As parents, it's easy to project our own dreams (and worries) onto our children and we begin to label them: easygoing, fussy, gentle, clingy, happy, feisty. When you catch yourself labeling your baby, stop and pray that God will reveal his greater design. He created your baby with the gifts and abilities that he will use for his glory. Take time this week to pray over your baby, thanking God for your child and who he created them to be.

## BABY *Bite*

My role as parent wasn't to "change" my child, either by controlling her problematic behaviors or rewarding more admirable ones. My role was to come alongside the Holy Spirit as he molded and shaped her into exactly the piece of art he created her to be.

We have the honor of preparing our children in ways big and small to do the work that God has already begun in them. Their unique gifts and challenges, their quirks and idiosyncrasies, the things we love most and struggle against – they are all part of the masterpiece God is revealing.

# TODDLER *Steps*

By your child's first birthday, you probably have a clearer snapshot of their interests and personality. Your toddler may even have words to further illustrate their temperament, sharing likes and dislikes, demands and protests, affection and frustration. They are also beginning to frame their understanding of self and how they fit in with the world around them, so the labels you give them – especially labels spoken aloud in their presence – have the power to become self-fulfilling prophecy. As you come alongside the work God is doing in their life, use your words to praise God's handiwork. The way they say "hi" to everyone in the store, or try so hard to complete a task, or give big hugs – these are small expressions of who God is shaping them to be. Pray that God will reveal his work in big and small ways, and take time with your child to thank God for who they are and who God is creating them to be.

# CHAPTER 21

# The Waiting – He is with Us

## 📖 MEDITATE

*"Surely the day is coming; it will burn like a furnace. All the arrogant and every evildoer will be stubble, and the day that is coming will set them on fire," says the LORD Almighty. "Not a root or a branch will be left to them. But for you who revere my name, the sun of righteousness will rise with healing in its rays.* – Malachi 4:1-2 (NIV)

Extended passage: Malachi 4:1-6

## ✏️ ANTICIPATE

● What did you feel when you discovered you would be a mother or father for the first time?

_____

_____

● How do you handle waiting?

_____

_____

"You're going to be a father." I remember a doctor looking me in the eye and confirming the news. In that thrilling moment, my body filled with adrenaline and I was ready to go. Let's have a baby! And in the weeks and months after hearing the news I filled my time with trips to the doctor, visits to the hardware and paint store, room decorating, hospital tours, parenting classes, and getting ready for the baby to arrive. There was constant action and conversation. But once the checklist was completed – all I could do was wait.

## THE WAITING

Not a whole lot gets done during the waiting. That's the point, you are waiting. The Bible was written in two parts or testaments. Malachi chapter 4 marks the end of the Old Testament. Matthew chapter 1 marks the beginning of the New Testament. But when you turn the page in your Bible from Malachi to Matthew, you might not realize the 400 year historical gap between the pages. Scholars call these 400 years the "Intertestamental" period, a time when God went silent, no prophets spoke in the land, and God's people were under the thumb of various foreign superpowers. A better word for "intertestamental" is simply, waiting. God's people were waiting a long time to hear him speak.

## THE WONDER

There will be moments when you feel as though God is silent. When you need to hear his voice and you come up empty. When you read his Word and nothing stands out. Is God here? Maybe you are facing this kind of difficult waiting on God right now. I want you to know I've been there. I've been the one waiting for God to answer my prayers for health or finances. I've been the one exhausted and tear-stained. God is with you. God is for you. God is present even in silence. God exists even though we cannot always see him at work. We need not wonder, for God is always near us in the waiting.

Photo © szefei

# BABY *Steps*

Moments of silence are rare in any home with an infant. But just because there's noise doesn't mean a quiet soul is impossible. So this week, find moments to quiet your soul. Wait on God. Sit in silence. In those times, reflect on the silence of God. Teach your baby to appreciate silence. One of the most profound moments of child development is how they work through separation anxiety. Infants do not understand you exist when they cannot see you. So when mom or dad leaves their sight, the child responds. This week, play Peek-a-Boo often. When you have to leave, reassure your baby with calming words. Say "I love you" and "I will come back."

## BABY *Bite*

There will be moments when you feel as though God is silent. When you need to hear his voice and you come up empty.

## TODDLER *Tips*

God exists even though we cannot always see him at work. We need not wonder, for God is always near us in the waiting.

# TODDLER *Steps*

Toddlers love to fill the silence. But noise doesn't necessarily prevent you from experiencing a quiet soul. Find moments to quiet your soul. Sit in silence, waiting on God and reflecting on the silence of God. Then teach your toddler to appreciate silence. This week, play hide and seek with your toddler. Hide and have them try to find you. Make your hiding place difficult so they have to really try to find you. Show them the place you were hiding and let them know you were there all along. Remind them of God's presence with them always.

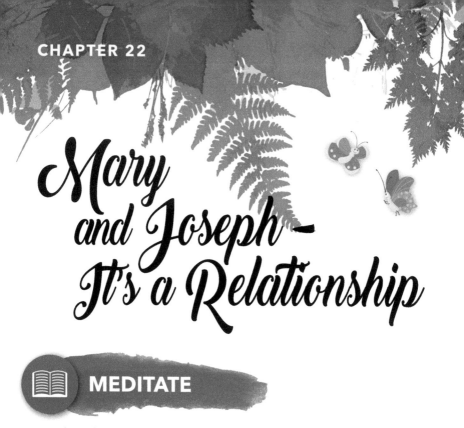

# CHAPTER 22

# Mary and Joseph – It's a Relationship

## 📖 MEDITATE

*But then the chosen time came. God sent his Son. A woman gave birth to him. He was born under the authority of the law. He came to set free those who were under the authority of the law. He wanted us to be adopted as children with all the rights children have.* – Galatians 4:4-5

Extended passage: Galatians 4:4-7

## ✏️ ANTICIPATE

● What was the last need your child had that you met?

_____

_____

_____

● What needs have you seen God meet this week?

_____

_____

I was seven months pregnant with my first child, singing carols by candlelight at our church's Christmas Eve service, celebrating one birth while waiting expectantly for another. I felt a new appreciation for Mary - for her faith in God's plan through twists and turns. I thought of Joseph, too, and how he must have felt awaiting the birth of a son that was not his own. Mary would have felt him kick and move, and I imagine she felt a deep connection to her unborn baby. But Joseph was disconnected physically and biologically from this child that he had been called to raise.

## PIVOTAL CHARACTERS

What an odd way to send the Messiah into the world. Whispers of scandal? Family drama? I wonder what prompted God to choose Mary and Joseph. We know that they were people of faith but Scripture doesn't reveal what made them stand out as potential parents of the Messiah. Whatever the reasons, God introduced them as pivotal characters in his story. He sent his Son to be their child, so that all of us could be adopted as his children. God sent Jesus to walk among us, so that we could walk as children of God.

## THE VALUE OF PARENTS

God chose to send his Son to be cared for by a mom and a dad, and then he chose to become our Father, inviting us into his family as children. What a clear sign that he values the work we do as moms and dads! And what a comforting reminder that he loves and cares for us, like a father loves and cares for his child. As a parent, I don't debate about *if* I should meet my children's needs (although I certainly become weary at times from the work!). I am called to care for them. And while it's my responsibility, it is also my joy. Being a parent has changed my perspective of God, and I have a new picture of God my Father. I know that I am loved, cherished, by a God who knows me and cares for my needs.

Photo © Dayna More

# BABY *Steps*

Babies give us endless opportunities to meet their needs in tangible ways. Unable to care for themselves, they depend on us for survival, and they are learning to trust us as we meet their needs. This week, demonstrate God's love as Father by responding to your baby's needs. As you complete the everyday tasks of feeding, clothing, diapering, comforting, and caring for your baby, tell them that you love and will take care of them, and that God will always love and care for them.

## BABY *Bite*

God sent Jesus to walk among us, so that we could walk as children of God. He chose to send his Son to be cared for by a mom and a dad, and then he chose to become our Father, inviting us into his family as children.

## TODDLER *Tips*

Knowing that he sees me as his child gives me great comfort. I know that I am loved, cherished, by a God who knows me and cares for my needs.

# TODDLER *Steps*

Having learned to trust that you will take care of them, your toddler is ready to set out and explore the world. They still need you to meet their basic needs, but now they need to develop some independence so they can learn to meet some of their needs on their own. You can meet this need for independence while still taking care of them by giving them safe places to explore while you sit back and observe. As they venture out, demonstrate God's love as Father by letting them know that you are right there with them. Encourage them to jump, climb, and explore in a safe environment, but be ready to offer help when they get stuck, and comfort when they get hurt. As you meet their needs – by encouraging independence and coming to the rescue – remind them that you love and will take care of them, and that God will always love and take care of them.

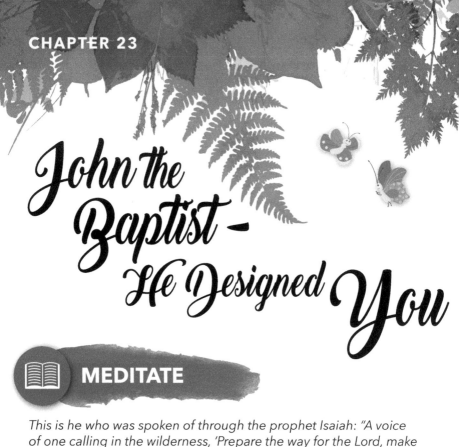

# CHAPTER 23

# John the Baptist – He Designed You

## MEDITATE

*This is he who was spoken of through the prophet Isaiah: "A voice of one calling in the wilderness, 'Prepare the way for the Lord, make straight paths for him.'"* – Matthew 3:3 (NIV)

Extended passage: Matthew 3:1-12

## ANTICIPATE

● How did God prepare you for being a parent?

_____

_____

_____

● What are you preparing your child to be?

_____

_____

_____

After getting married, I made a list of all the financial things needing to fall into place before we would have any children. If we could fill the emergency fund, get rid of the car payment, and pay down the student loans we would be ready. When Warren Buffet and Dave Ramsey called to congratulate us on our fiscal responsibility, then and only then would we be ready to have a baby.

Spoiler alert. They never called.

## REVELATION

I realized: You are never fully ready to have a baby. It comes before you are ready. Every time. But in God's Story, the timing was perfect for Jesus' arrival on earth. Every word from Genesis forward points to the Messiah. And part of the perfect timing of God bringing Jesus to earth involved a man named John.

God used John to prepare the way for Jesus' ministry and message. John is referred to as "John the Baptist" because crowds would travel to the wilderness to hear John's preaching, confess their sins, and be baptized in the Jordan River. He is possibly the weirdest person in the Bible. The picture painted of John the Baptist is like Gandalf meets Ron Swanson meets Survivor Man.

## ONE STRANGE DUDE

John the Baptist lived in the desert. He made the Paleo food plan look tame with his regular diet of locusts and wild honey. John's clothing was rough camel-hide garments. By all accounts, this man was strange. Strange habits. Odd style. Yet we read John the Baptist was a man sent from God for a purpose.

John was preparing the way for Jesus, pointing people to repentance. Despite all of his uniqueness, Jesus tells us "among those born of women there is no one greater than John" (Luke 7:28). John's story tells us that God can use unexpected things to prepare the way for the most important things.

Photo © Gelpi

# BABY *Steps*

I've read that 95% of parenting is getting your kids ready to go somewhere (the other 5% is asking them to turn off the lights). As you get your baby ready this week, reflect on John the Baptist's story and be grateful. We have the extraordinary gift of being on the other side of Jesus' death and resurrection. The Story of God's redemption and love in Jesus, prepared by John the Baptist, gives each of us access to a relationship with God for eternity. We have so much to be grateful for when we look at The Story. But our days are not spent reflecting on God's Story; they are spent in the laundry room, the workplace, the kitchen, and the car. Gratitude is essential to defending our hearts from complaining and discontentment while anchoring us in thankfulness for all God has prepared for us. Express gratitude for what God has provided. Babies divert from the schedule with regularity. Use these moments to be filled with thankfulness.

## BABY *Bite*

In God's Story, the timing was perfect for Jesus's arrival on earth. Every word from Genesis forward points to the Messiah. And part of the perfect timing of God bringing Jesus to earth involved a man named John.

## TODDLER *Tips*

John's story tells us that God can use unexpected things to prepare the way for the most important things.

# TODDLER *Steps*

Toddlers are infamous for the stubborn streaks, and to parents who give their time and energy to their child's care, it's easy to become frustrated with our toddler's apparent lack of gratitude for our sacrifice. But we, too, are often ungrateful. This side of God's Story, thousands of years after John the Baptist prepared the way for Jesus to serve and sacrifice so that we could experience a relationship with God for eternity, we get so caught up in our daily work that we forget the gift of God's redemptive work. We lose The Story when we get bogged down with the day-to-day details. This week, integrate gratitude throughout your daily routine. Surround your life with gratitude and express it to God. Draw your toddler's attention to things, places, experiences, and gifts God has provided for them. Encourage them to identify the things they can be thankful for.

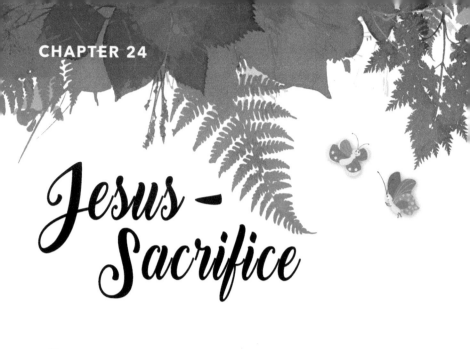

# CHAPTER 24

# Jesus – Sacrifice

## MEDITATE

*Here is what love is. It is not that we loved God. It is that he loved us and sent his Son to give his life and pay for our sins.* – 1 John 4:10

Extended passage: 1 John 4:7-12

## ANTICIPATE

● How closely did labor follow your birth plan?

_____

_____

_____

● What sacrifices have you made for your children because you love them?

_____

_____

_____

It was more than a week before my due date when I went into labor with my first baby. I arrived at the hospital armed with my Birth Plan, ready for labor and delivery. Then complications led to more complications...but throughout the entire ordeal, my concern was always for my baby. So when the doctor looked at me and told me that I needed an emergency c section because my baby was in distress, I didn't ask what would happen to me – I asked if my baby would be ok. And when I heard her first cry, and then the news that she was perfect, I cried tears of joy. Laying on an operating table, with a long recovery in front of me, I could only think of her. I would think of my Birth Plan later, and mourn its unraveling. But in the end, the only part of my plan that I truly valued was the part where she arrived safely into this world. In the end, I didn't give a second thought when I had to make sacrifices so we could be together.

## WHAT LOVE IS

God loving us, and proving it by sending his Son – by sacrificing a part of himself – is the ultimate definition of love. We like to touch and see and experience things, and so the God who IS love sends Jesus because love is more than a concept or an emotion. The person of Jesus walked this earth as God's greatest act of love. "For God so loved that he gave," John 3:16 tells us. Jesus is the most powerful example of God's love for us.

## THE GREATEST SACRIFICE

As parents, we often make sacrifices for our children – whether those sacrifices affect our birth plan or budget or zip code, we make them out of love for our children. But God's sacrifice was far greater than anything we can imagine. God's plan was always for us to be together, and when his plan unraveled, God sent Jesus as the ultimate act of love so that in the end, together is exactly where we would be.

# BABY *Steps*

Babies require their parents to make sacrifices every day. We sacrifice time, money, sleep, comfort, and more to meet their needs. Think of the sacrifices you've made in the past 24 hours alone, so that your baby could be fed, clothed, and cared for. These simple acts can help illustrate how God showed his love for us by sending Jesus. This week, every time you make a sacrifice to meet your baby's needs, tell your baby that you love them. As you do, thank God for sending Jesus as God's sacrifice, sent to demonstrate God's love for you.

## BABY *Bite*

God loving us, and proving it by sending his Son – by sacrificing a part of himself – is the ultimate definition of love.

## TODDLER *Tips*

God's plan was always for us to be together, and when his plan unraveled, God sent Jesus as the ultimate act of love so that in the end, together is exactly where we would be.

# TODDLER *Steps*

Toddlers are becoming more independent, but still require their parents to sacrifice a great deal to take care of them. What sacrifices have you made today so that you could meet your toddler's needs? These sacrifices can illustrate how God's sacrifice - Jesus - shows us that God loves us. This week, as you make sacrifices to care for your toddler, let them know what you are doing and why. Say something like, "Today I woke up early to make you breakfast because I love you." Then add, "God sent Jesus to show us that he loves us." Before bed, thank God for sending Jesus so we could know God and know that he loves us.

# CHAPTER 25

# The Disciples Share the Story

## 📖 MEDITATE

*Therefore go and make disciples of all nations, baptizing them in the name of the Father and of the Son and of the Holy Spirit, and teaching them to obey everything I have commanded you. And surely I am with you always, to the very end of the age.* – Matthew 28:19-20 (NIV)

Extended passage: Matthew 28:16-20

## ✏️ ANTICIPATE

● What instructions do you remember your mom or dad repeating to you as a child?

_____

_____

_____


● How has your child surprised you?

_____

_____

My daughter Sofia is the comedian of the family. She has shared so many funny quips with us, we created a hashtag for her: #classicsofi. One afternoon I was alone with Sofia at our house on a Saturday. I knew I had a lot of work to do around the house so I starting ticking off my checklist. Fix the closet shelf. Clean the windows. Dust the furniture. I checked off a dozen things on my to-do list.

## 1000 TOYS

After some time passed, I realized my daughter Sofia had used this time to play with 1000 toys – which were now all over the floor in the living room. Knowing I had more things on my checklist and the mess needed to be cleaned up, I gave Sofia simple instructions, "Would you take all of these toys back upstairs?" Like always, Sofia cheerfully replied, "Ok Dad."

I kept a closer eye on my toddler as I continued to work around the house and she made the short trip up and down the stairs to put away her things. When I finished my checklist, we had a snack and headed upstairs for nap time. At the top of the stairs I noticed all of the toys were there. You could barely pass through the pile of stuffed animals and dolls, it was all right at the top of the stairs.

"Sofie," I began, "Why didn't you do what I asked you to do?" "I did what you asked me Dad." She replied, "I took all the toys back upstairs."

#classicsofi

## SHARE THE STORY

Jesus gave some instructions to his followers before he ascended into heaven. Jesus told them to, "Go and make disciples." He called them to carry the story – the Gospel – all over the world. His instructions were crystal clear: This Story that has been entrusted to you is not your own. Go tell it to other people. You are reading this book because of Jesus' instruction to his disciples. Somewhere along the way, you were told about who Jesus is and what he has done. And now you get to share this story with your kids.

Photo © Oksana Kuzmina

# BABY *Steps*

While your baby is not going to understand and follow directions, they need to hear your voice and understand how something goes from start to finish. While they cannot yet follow detailed instructions, they are learning to understand the world around then and how to respond to the words we use. This week, rehearse the common things you do around the house and in the car with your infant. If you're cooking, voice the steps out loud. If you're driving, share the journey's turns. Give your infant a sense of beginning and end.

## BABY *Bite*

Jesus gave some instructions to his followers before he ascended into heaven. Jesus told them to, "Go and make disciples."

Somewhere along the way, you were told about who Jesus is and what he has done. And now you get to share this story with your kids.

# TODDLER *Steps*

Toddlers can follow simple, one-step instructions, and can begin learning to follow two or even three-step instructions as they get closer to the preschool years. As they learn to listen to our words, the instructions we give them are important. Practice giving instructions to your toddler this week. Be clear and specific. Cheer them on as they listen and respond. Learn to give one instruction at a time. Toddlers are capable of learning two-step directions, but they need practice! During your practice, remind them of Jesus' instructions to his disciples.

# CHAPTER 26

# Paul – Expect the Unexpected

## 📖 MEDITATE

*But the Lord said to Ananias, "Go! This man is my chosen instrument to proclaim my name to the Gentiles and their kings and to the people of Israel.* – Acts 9:15 (NIV)

Extended passage: Acts 9:1-18

## ✏️ ANTICIPATE

● Describe a place you love to go with your family.

_____

_____

_____

● What story do you love to tell about your kids?

_____

_____

_____

The gap between not having children and being a parent is miles wide. It's why parents of a newborn bristle when a puppy owner says, "I know what you're going through." You don't. You have a dog. I have a human. End of story. For me the expectations gap was significant. I thought all of my children would be boys. Instead, we have three girls and one boy. I thought all of our children would be easy. My oldest daughter had colic and cried uncontrollably. My youngest daughter struggles to be put down for naps and bedtime. I never realized how much I would enjoy the evening routine or teaching my kids things. I was completely unprepared for how many diapers two children under two required.

## UNEXPECTED JOURNEY

The bottom line? Parenting was an unexpected journey, a wild ride I was unprepared for and have struggled through yet loved. And when I read the Bible I am reminded of many moments in the story where God used unprepared, overwhelmed people. Moses had a speech problem. Elijah had a pity party. David was a shepherd. Jonah ran. Thomas doubted. And the list goes on. In Acts 9, Paul (who is also called Saul throughout the book) was antagonizing those who followed the teachings of Jesus. And on the way to Damascus, God met Paul on the road and began to speak to him. In that moment Paul's life changed.

## A BIGGER STORY

God shifted the trajectory of Paul's life and gave him the mission to proclaim the good news of Jesus. Paul did not expect this or plan for this, but God brought it to pass. God chose him. God sent him and gave him a story to tell. And the same is true for you and me. We have been chosen by God to participate in a bigger story, something larger than ourselves and our families. And we get the privilege of sharing that story with our children.

Photo © Africa Studio

# BABY

Becoming a parent is a game-changer. All parents find themselves overwhelmed at times, especially in those first weeks and months as they learn to read and respond to their baby's cries. Are you unprepared or under equipped for your role as a parent? Look back at the list of men and women God used in the Bible who were just like you. Now think of what God accomplished through them. Moses led God's people out of Egypt. Elijah performed miracles and humiliated the prophets of Baal. David was Israel's greatest king. Jonah led the people of Nineveh to God. Peter preached at Pentecost. Thomas brought the message of the gospel to modern day India. This week, dream of how God might use your child to accomplish his purposes. Think through the plans and story he will unfold in your child's life. Encourage your infant in moments of pause this week with these words, "God has a plan for your life."

BABY

When I read the Bible I am reminded of many moments in the story where God used unprepared, overwhelmed people.

TODDLER *Tips*

We have been chosen by God to participate in a bigger story, something larger than ourselves and our families. And we get the privilege of sharing that story with our children.

# TODDLER *Steps*

As babies grow into toddlers, parents are faced with new and ever-changing challenges that can be frustrating or overwhelming at times. Do you find yourself struggling to keep up with the demands of parenting your toddler? Look to Scripture for examples of people just like you – men and women God used to accomplish great things. Moses led God's people out of Egypt. Elijah performed miracles and humiliated the prophets of Baal. David was Israel's greatest king. Jonah led the people of Nineveh to God. Peter preached at Pentecost. Thomas brought the message of the gospel to modern day India. Paul was a man God prepared to share his story with others. This week, use stories to encourage your toddler. Read an extra Bible story. Pull out one more book before bedtime. Spend time reveling in story together. Remember to share Paul's story of God using someone who expected one thing and receiving something bigger.

# Respond with Praise

## MEDITATE

*"For you created my inmost being; you knit me together in my mother's womb. I praise you because I am fearfully and wonderfully made; your works are wonderful, I know that full well."* – Psalm 139:13-14 (NIV)

Extended passage: Psalm 139:1-8

## ANTICIPATE

● How do you enjoy expressing praise to God?

_____

_____

_____

● What three things do you love most about your child?

_____

_____

_____

Pregnancy is amazing. It can be difficult and even scary, but tracking the development of your baby as they grow inside the womb is bearing witness to a miracle. I'll never forget hearing that first heartbeat and the relief and joy that flooded my heart. And then seeing tiny legs kicking during a sonogram, feeling elbows jab against my ribs, and the bizarre sense of each baby hiccuping inside my womb. Psalm 139 came alive to me in those moments, as I envisioned the creator of mountains and oceans doing the intricate work of knitting together a precious life inside of me.

## HIS WORK IS WONDERFUL

It gave me joy during an easy pregnancy, it gave me peace during a difficult one, and it gave me hope and eventually healing, even in the pain of pregnancy lost. Each of these babies was knit together by a Creator that loved them. And while the brokenness of the places outside sometimes reaches in and brings brokenness to the places within, God is still a God to be praised. His work is still wonderful, even if we have to wait until Heaven to see it.

## I PRAISE YOU

Cradling a newborn, it's easy to see that they are fearfully and wonderfully made. And then the sleepless nights string together and the endless tasks of feeding and diapering and rocking become wearisome. No matter how much I loved my babies, I have to admit that at times I lost sight of God's wonderful work and the only thing I knew full well was that I was nearly at my limit. Psalm 139 beckons to weary parents – "look to the God who knit you together. Praise him. Know *full well* that his works are wonderful." As parents, it's easy to focus on our body's struggles. Our brains are fuzzy, our nerves frayed, our backs achy, our skin stretched and saggy. But our inmost being was created by God and from that place we must respond with praise. May you look with fresh eyes this week at your child and at yourself, seeing that you both are a wonderful work of God, and may you be prompted to respond with praise.

Photo © Vitalinka

# BABY *Steps*

Your baby grows and develops by astounding leaps and bounds in the first year. Take a moment to think of the ways your baby has grown and developed since birth. God was at work, knitting them together in your womb to prepare them for the world and creating the intricate systems that would continue developing outside the womb. Hold your baby close, taking time to recognize and appreciate how God has created them. Then let your baby listen as you respond in praise - sing or pray, giving God praise for his wonderful works.

## BABY *Bite*

Cradling a newborn, it's easy to see that they are fearfully and wonderfully made; it's impossible not to see God's work as wonderful in those early moments when our eyes are fresh with wonder.

Appreciate the way God created your child, taking time to consider that God created those things you know and love about them.

## TODDLER *Steps*

Toddlers are becoming more aware of their bodies and love naming body parts. Sit your toddler in front of a mirror. Let them study themselves, and as they do, take a moment to think of how your toddler has grown and developed since birth. Appreciate the way God created them, taking time to consider that God created those things you know and love about them. Then help your toddler name their body parts. Say, "this is your arm – God made your arm!" Continue as long as your toddler is enjoying the game, and then when you are finished, praise God together. Sing a song of praise, or say a simple prayer praising God for his wonderful work.

# CHAPTER 28

# Respond with Prayer

## MEDITATE

*"So pray to the LORD your God. Pray that he'll tell us where we should go. Pray that he'll tell us what we should do."* – Jeremiah 42:3

Extended passage: Jeremiah 42:1-43:4

## ANTICIPATE

● Have you ever wandered off a road or trail and gotten lost? How did you find your way back?

_____

_____

_____

● How have you wandered away from God's path or plan recently?

_____

_____

_____

## ♥ RELATE

Toddlers are infamous for using the phrase "Me do it!" As parents, it's our job to navigate when to step in and when to foster independence. When my oldest learned to walk, she absolutely despised sitting in the stroller. So I broke down and bought one of those stuffed animal backpacks with a leash...and she LOVED it. She'd run back and forth, sometimes tugging to go just a bit farther. That tug always reminded me that my bright-eyed curious toddler was prone to wander.

### PRONE TO WANDER

I'm reminded of a line from the hymn "Come Thou Fount": "prone to wander, Lord I feel it, prone to leave the God I love." If I'm being honest, in my deepest heart I am a wanderer. I love to blaze my own trail, and I often forget that being a Christ-follower means that I follow instead of lead. The Israelites were no different and here we find them in some hot water, so they turn to Jeremiah, God's appointed prophet, and beseech him to pray on their behalf. If you read the rest of the chapter, God speaks to Jeremiah and points the way but the the Israelites hear God's instructions and then do the opposite. What God does in this passage is answer. I used to wonder why passages like this were included in Scripture – God speaking truth and foretelling sin and the inevitable consequences. But if the Word reveals who God is, then stories like this paint a picture of a God who is willing to guide even when he knows we are slow to follow. Because in showing us the path, he shows us how to return. He points the way back from where we wandered to where we belong.

### GUIDING THE WAY

As a parent, it's our responsibility to guide our children on the right path. That's a daunting task, considering we are sinners with a tendency to wander off the path ourselves. But our wanderings can teach our children that God directs our paths, and he is waiting and willing to guide us back to him every time. If you're a wanderer (and we all are), then respond with prayer, knowing that God will always answer.

Photo © wong sze yuen

# BABY *Steps*

Babies learn to recognize their parent's voice while still in the womb. They instinctively turn toward your voice from the moment they are born. As they begin rolling around, crawling, and eventually walking, they will often look back toward you to see if they're still there, watching out for them. You can model that God is always there, ready to listen when we pray, by telling your baby "I'm still here!" when they look back for you. Remind them often that God is here for them, too, and take time to pray and thank God for his presence with you and your baby.

## BABY *Bite*

But if the Word reveals who God is, then stories like Jeremiah's paint a picture of a God who is willing to guide even when he knows we are slow to follow.

## TODDLER *Tips*

As a parent, it's our responsibility to guide our children on the right path.

# TODDLER *Steps*

Toddlers are eager to explore and are more comfortable moving beyond your arms' reach and even your sight. But they will often check back, looking to see if you are still there, watching out for them. The next time you take them to a park or indoor play area, watch to see how often they look back to you. Wave and tell them, "I'm still here!" Later, tell them that just like you were there when they looked for you, God will always be there for them, too. Pray with your toddler, thanking God that he is always there.

# CHAPTER 29

# Respond with Silence

## 📖 MEDITATE

*This is what the Sovereign L*ORD*, the Holy One of Israel, says:*
   *"In repentance and rest is your salvation,*
   *in quietness and trust is your strength,*
   *but you would have none of it.* – 1 John 4:7-8 (NIV)

Extended passage: Isaiah 30:15-18

## ✏️ ANTICIPATE

● When your house is quiet, what do you spend time doing?

_____

_____

_____

● How do you respond to silence?

_____

_____

_____

By far, the toughest thing about parenting a young child is the radical change to your sleep schedule. I'm a diva. I need my beauty rest.

Just kidding.

When a baby or toddler continually wakes up and needs to be fed, cuddled, changed, and put back to sleep, the waking inevitably impacts mom or dad. As an infant, my daughter Isabel struggled to sleep. Now being a parent is a survival exercise. You do whatever you can to make it. If your baby will not sleep in the crib but will fall asleep in a shoebox, you go with the shoebox. If the $300 bouncer you got at the baby shower makes the baby cry when you put her in it, but when you put her in upside down she loves it – you go upside down. Every time.

## COLIC

When it came to getting Isabel to sleep, I did whatever I could to help quiet my fussing, colicky baby. When she would only sleep in the car, I would drive for hours. For weeks I walked in circles around our tiny condo holding her and listening to music. She would cry and scream for hours. Midnight. 1am. 3am. I would put on Ray Charles and listen to "Georgia on My Mind", "Hit the Road Jack", and "Mess Around". I'm pretty sure she cracked a smile every time we got to "The Night Time Is the Right Time." Eventually she would fall asleep in my arms and we would crash on the couch.

## QUIET

When we read Isaiah 30:15, we discover how much God desires for us to be quiet. He's the one trying to calm us and reassure us while we are the crying infant. The prophet Isaiah shares "in quietness and trust is your strength, but you would have none of it." How often do we choose noise over quiet? I know how difficult it can be to find quiet moments in our homes, but silence provides strength while noise erodes it. Somehow Isaiah was able to be quiet enough to hear God's voice speak and we can do the same.

Photo © Gelpi

# BABY *Steps*

We often think of praying as talking to God, but communication involves listening as well as speaking. When we are silent, God will often speak to our hearts. This week, take time to hold your sleeping infant and enjoy the silence. During these times, release the pressure to accomplish something or make something happen. Just sit in silence and listen. What does the Holy Spirit reveal to you in these moments? Reflect with another parent about your experience of silence and what you learn.

## BABY *Bite*

When we read Isaiah 30:15, we discover how much God desires for us to be quiet. He's the one trying to calm us and reassure us while we are the crying infant.

## TODDLER *Tips*

Being a parent is a survival exercise. You do whatever you can to survive the island. In order to make it, you try everything possible to stay alive.

# TODDLER *Steps*

Toddlers are busy and not often quiet. As a result, our home is often filled with noise and lacking in silence. Our prayers are often the same - filled with words with no space for silence. But it is in silence that God speaks to us. This week, before you go to sleep, go into your toddler's room and pick them up. Appreciate the silence and be mindful of what the Holy Spirit is revealing to you. Post a picture on social media and share what you experienced in this mindful moment.

# CHAPTER 30

# Respond with Joy

## MEDITATE

*"My brothers and sisters, you will face all kinds of trouble. When you do, think of it as pure joy."* – James 1:2

Extended passage: James 2:2-18

## ANTICIPATE

● What was the most difficult hardship you've ever faced?

_____

_____

_____

● What did it teach you?

_____

_____

_____

Shortly after my second daughter was born, our family struggled financially. I prayed fervently for God to provide stability; to secure the job I already had so we could remain stable in the place we already were. Months of job uncertainty turned into a long job hunt, which eventually led us to relocate. Over a year later, with two toddlers in tow, we settled into a place where everything was new and unfamiliar. It would be another year or so before we felt like we were home and this season of difficulty had passed.

## LOOKING BACK

As I think back, I can tell you I considered that season anything but "pure joy." I wish I could sit down next to the younger version of myself and share what I've learned along the way – that yes, there would be hard years, but those hardships will make you stronger. They will make you a better follower of Christ and leader of little feet that follow in your footsteps. I know that now because I learned it along the way. It's the journey that teaches us, and God uses the difficult paths to make us into who we're meant to be. James writes of trouble as an inevitability and then tells the reader to think of it as pure joy. Like so many truths in Scripture, it seems a bit upside down.

## DISCOVERING JOY

Verse 4 goes on to say that "you must allow this strength to finish its work. Then you will be all you should be. You will have everything you need." During those difficult years, I prayed for God to fix everything, because it's what I thought I needed. But reading and reflecting on James 1, I know now that going through the struggle was the only way to get what I really needed. And what I really needed was joy found in all circumstances (even struggles), because it's found in my Father. Struggles still come and go, and joy isn't always my first response But I have learned to walk the difficult paths and consider them pure joy as I look forward to the places they will take me, and as I trust my Father to guide me through.

# BABY *Steps*

As babies grow, developmental milestones are often accompanied by uncomfortable symptoms. In a sense, they struggle as they grow. They may sleep less when learning a new skill, become frustrated or irritable before learning to crawl, and feel pain as their teeth come in. During those difficult days, we comfort and care for them and sympathize with their struggles, but we wouldn't dream of wishing them to remain helpless infants forever. When they discover their hands, crawl for the first time, or show us their first toothy grin, we take photos and videos and we clap and cheer. We celebrate the milestones that emerge from a struggle. The next time your baby struggles through a stage of development; consider the milestone that is coming. Care for your baby, considering it pure joy, and then celebrate the milestone that follows, thanking God for the way he created your baby to learn and grow.

## BABY *Bite*

The next time your baby struggles through a stage of development; consider the milestone that is coming.

# TODDLER *Steps*

Toddlers also experience struggles that propel them into the next milestone. Many of these struggles revolve around their developing independence – wanting to do things for themselves – and they are better able to vocalize their feelings as they struggle. Empathize with their struggle while encouraging them to consider their struggle as joy. Say, "it's hard to put on your shoes. You are a big kid and want to learn. I'm proud of you for trying!" Take time to teach your toddler a new "big kid" skill and celebrate their milestone together. Remind them that they worked hard to learn their new skill, and that God made their body to learn and grow.

# CHAPTER 31

# Respond with Lament

## MEDITATE

*I cry aloud to the Lord; I lift up my voice to the Lord for mercy.*
*I pour out before him my complaint; before him I tell my trouble.*
– Psalm 142:1-2 (NIV)

Extended passage: Psalm 142:1-7

## ANTICIPATE

● When was the last time you were completely overwhelmed?

_____

_____

_____

● How do you respond in times like this?

_____

_____

_____

## ❤️ RELATE

Several years ago my wife asked me if I would be willing to open our home to kids in crisis. She felt called and convicted to use our home as a place kids in need could find love and safety. It looked like a wonderful program making the difference in the lives of many children in our community. I just didn't want any part of it. I had all the excuses lined up. And they were good. We already had two young kids. I was a children's pastor, spending weekends at the church for services helping countless families. Our tiny duplex was cramped, how could we fit another person inside? With my excuses protecting me, I was unashamedly the lone holdout. We simply could not take in any children.

## SPEAK

Then one day in the car after meeting up with a close friend for coffee, I felt like I heard the Holy Spirit speak to me. This is not something I typically experience on my ride to work. But I heard from the Holy Spirit, sitting in my Chevy Malibu, asking me "Matt, who does your house belong to?" I responded out loud, "My house belongs to me. My name is on the mortgage. I pay the bank every month." God spoke again, "Matt, who does your family belong to?" I replied "My family belongs to me. I'm the father. I'm the breadwinner. I pay the bills and take care of them." "No. Your family is my beloved treasure. Your home is my gift to you. Use this gift for others.

## LAMENT

Of the 150 chapters in the book of Psalms, Bible scholars identify over a third as psalms of lament. Another word for lament is complaining. These psalms are simply complaints before God. Psalm 142 is among them and its writer David pens, "I pour out before him my complaint; before him I tell my trouble." God invites us to respond to him in the difficult moments of our lives with raw and authentic words, inviting God into the trouble and placing our trust in him alone.

Photo © AlohaHawaii

# BABY *Steps*

As a parent, there will be rough moments when you are ready to throw in the towel. Maybe you experienced one this morning. A moment when you are finished. Done. When you can't even. Babies experience this too, but they express their feelings nonverbally. This week as you notice these nonverbal cues, assign words to them. "You're feeling sad because you need a diaper change." "You're feeling grumpy because you are hungry." "You're feeling hurt because your teeth are coming in." In each instance, invite God into the admission and model what it looks like to trust God with the way we feel.

## BABY *Bite*

God invites us to respond to him in the difficult moments of our lives with raw and authentic words, inviting God into the trouble and placing our trust in him alone.

## TODDLER *Tips*

As a parent, there will be rough moments when you are ready to throw in the towel. These are the moments to invite God into the mess.

# TODDLER *Steps*

When we vulnerably come to God, we slowly begin to recognize our faith is stronger than the doubts our difficulties ask of it. We allow the difficult circumstances we face to submit to God's power and turn our hearts toward praise. Toddlers experience a wide range of emotions and a lot of their frustration comes from an inability to voice their feelings. This week, help your toddler learn to label their feelings. When they are upset, help them finish the sentence "I feel mad because…" When they are angry, help them finish the phrase, "I feel angry because…" If they struggle, ask your toddler if they need you to give them some ideas. As your child labels what they feel, teach them to give their feelings to God.

# CHAPTER 32

# Respond with Trust

## MEDITATE

*Trust in the Lord with all your heart*
  *and lean not on your own understanding;*
*in all your ways submit to him,*
  *and he will make your paths straight.* – Proverbs 3:5-6 NIV

Extended passage: Proverbs 3:1-18

## ANTICIPATE

● What kinds of advice did you receive when you had a baby?

_____

_____

_____

● When has the path of your life veered into an unforeseen direction?

_____

_____

_____

_____

There is no shortage of advice when you are getting ready to have a child. Before we had our children, we received such wisdom as: If you want to have a girl, eat broccoli and oranges. If you want to have a boy, eat bananas and spinach. Add rice cereal to a bottle at night to help babies sleep longer. If your baby is struggling to sleep at night, flip them head over heels to reset their internal clock. For good health, a baby should always taste their own bath water. I cannot make this stuff up.

## WHAT TO EXPECT

My first two children were born before smartphones, social media, and blogs. In order to get information about pregnancy, you needed to go to a bookstore or library and pick up a book. The book everyone recommended was *What to Expect When You're Expecting*. This book has sold over 18 million copies, been translated into 30 languages, and has become a mainstay for parents. I read the book cover to cover. With all of the advice being thrown my way, I needed something I could trust. Especially when the sleep struggles began, I *almost* caved and did the baby flip thing. All right I'll admit it. I did the baby flip thing and it didn't work.

## ONE VOICE

Through the surprising journey that is pregnancy and parenthood, we hear so many voices along the way. Among the many voices trying to get our attention and direct our steps, one voice must ring louder than all the rest. It is the voice of our heavenly Father, speaking to you and me through the power of the Holy Spirit. Will you trust God no matter through every surprise and unexpected twist in your journey? Through growth spurts, emergency room visits, first words, crawling and walking, illness, and hugs when you do not expect them? One of the many foundational truths we learn about God is he can be trusted. We can submit our journey to God himself and he will make the path straight.

Photo © Artem Furman

# BABY *Steps*

While babies lack the verbal communication skills to express how they are feeling, they use other tools to get your attention. By meeting your baby's needs, you are setting the stage for how your child will trust you and trust God. As your baby develops, be mindful of the sounds they make. Trust your instincts and attach sounds you hear regularly with a need. Certain cries often indicate specific needs like feeding, changing, or sleeping. As you attend and respond to the sounds, you are encouraging your baby to trust you.

### BABY *Bite*

Pregnancy and parenting are filled with surprises and there is no way to prepare for them.

## TODDLER *Tips*

Among the many voices trying to get our attention and direct our steps, one voice must ring louder than all the rest. It is the voice of our heavenly Father, speaking to you and me through the power of the Holy Spirit.

# TODDLER *Steps*

Toddlers are learning to express their thoughts and feelings with language, but they are still highly sensitive to stress and anxiety, which can be difficult for them to voice. This week, take a walk. Be intentional with your time, and invest in deepening the bond between you and your child. As you laugh and play together with your toddler, you are reinforcing the trust they have in you. Remind them in the middle of surprises how God is in control.

# CHAPTER 33

# Respond with Confession

## 📖 MEDITATE

*But God is faithful and fair. If we confess our sins, he will forgive our sins. He will forgive every wrong thing we have done. He will make us pure.*

— 1 John 1:9

Extended passage: 1 John 1

## ✏️ ANTICIPATE

● What is an area of sin that you struggle with?

_____

_____

_____

● What comes to mind when you think of confession?

_____

_____

_____

I used to be a parenting expert. And then? I had kids. It's so much easier to be a parenting expert before you have your own children. Holding my baby girl in my arms taught me in an instant that being responsible for a tiny person that you love more than life itself changes everything. Your attachment to your child obliterates any objectivity and sometimes makes it impossible to maintain perspective. Becoming a parent also shines a giant spotlight on our flaws. I was a far more calm and collected person when I hadn't been up all night with an inconsolable baby, before I had two toddlers requiring more attention than I had to spare. I felt like a glass that had been knocked over, and everything spilling out was ugly. My girls deserved better, and I would often pray desperately that God would make me more calm and patient, but in the heat of a bad moment I would tip like the glass and the words or the tone or the look on my face revealed a sinful heart spilling ugliness again.

## SIN AND CONFESSION

I had seen my impatience and short temper as a problem I should solve, but truth be told it was just plain old sin. I turned to my Father, who John describes so comfortingly as faithful and fair. I confessed my sin and I asked for forgiveness. And then I acknowledged my deep need for God to step in and take the ugliness that spilled when my cup was bumped, and make it pure and clean. I asked that the next time I found myself in a heated moment, God would simply prompt me to call on him.

## FORGIVENESS

Years later, I still sin but I've learned that parenting is a process, and you don't become an expert on a journey you haven't even completed. I have learned that parenting is much more about letting my Father teach me than it is about me teaching my children. When I fall short, I respond by confessing my sin to a Father who is fair and faithful, and who promises to forgive me and make me pure.

Photo © Paul Hakimata Photography

# BABY *Steps*

As parents, we want the best for our children, and holding our baby close, it's easy to feel like we don't measure up. That they deserve better. But what they need most is a parent who will show them what to do and where to turn when they make mistakes. They need a parent who models confession so they know that they have a God who offers forgiveness. This week, when you sin, confess it immediately. Let your baby hear you respond with confession and tell them that God is fair and faithful to forgive.

## BABY *Bite*

Your attachment to your child obliterates any objectivity and sometimes makes it impossible to maintain perspective.

## TODDLER *Tips*

Parenting is a process, and you don't become an expert on a journey you haven't even completed.

# TODDLER *Steps*

Toddlers are always watching us - they learn from what we do more than from what we say. Use your mistakes as an opportunity to teach your toddler about confession and forgiveness. When you sin this week, confess your sin immediately and ask God to forgive you. Make it a natural part of your daily rhythms and if your toddler is nearby, explain with simple words what you are doing: "I made a mistake when I got angry. I told God 'I'm sorry' and he loves me so he forgave me." When your toddler sins, encourage them to confess by saying, "I'm sorry" to God, then remind them that God will always forgive them.

# CHAPTER 34

# Respond with Gratitude

## 📖 MEDITATE

*Give thanks no matter what happens. God wants you to thank him because you believe in Christ Jesus."* – 1 Thessalonians 5:18

Extended passage: 1 Thessalonians 5:12-28

## ✏️ ANTICIPATE

● What are you most grateful for?

_____

_____

_____

● In what ways do you express thanks to God??

_____

_____

_____

_____

I was headed on a vacation a few days after I had found out I was pregnant with my third child, a long awaited answer to prayer after many months of struggling with infertility. As I boarded that flight I was filled with joy, grateful that my prayer had finally been answered. Ironically, the book I brought along focused on gratitude, and I was moved by words that echoed 1 Thessalonians 5:18 - *"give thanks no matter what happens."*

## NO MATTER WHAT HAPPENS

A day later I sat listening to a doctor explain "miscarriage" in clinical terms. I thought of the words I had read earlier that day, remembering my conviction to give thanks *no matter what happens*. First Thessalonians 5:18 goes on to tell us that our thanks is based on our belief in Christ, faith that isn't dependent on circumstances, no matter how difficult. In the days that followed, I practiced gratitude only by the grace of God. I practiced initially out of obedience but soon my practice began to form a habit, and obedience gave way to greater faith. I gave thanks for God's presence and comfort, for his hand at work in ways I didn't understand.

## GRATITUDE HEALS

What I learned from those days and months I practiced giving thanks, was that gratitude soothed the ache and I could feel it heal me from the inside out. Like most of God's commands, he gives them to us because he loves us and knows what we need. My heart still hurts for the child I lost. But it also gives thanks to the God who comforted me then and comforts me still. Almost a year after I sat in that hospital room grieving life lost, I held my baby boy in another hospital room celebrating life given. His birth didn't erase my grief, but it also reminded me that grief met with gratitude has the potential for breathing life into even the darkest places. My story would have more moments of grief and celebration, and in each of them I have learned to give thanks, no matter what happens, because I believe in Christ.

Photo © Marina Dyakonova

# BABY *Steps*

Babies absorb language from the time they are in the womb. They learn that words have meaning not just by what we say but by how we say it. You can begin teaching your baby gratitude by making the words "thank you" familiar, and conveying gratitude with your tone of voice. You can even teach them the sign for "thank you." Thank God for your child's love when you lay them down to sleep; thank God for food as you feed them; thank God for "mama" or "dada" as you hold them. Remember to give thanks even in difficult times – thank God for a soft blanket wrapped around them when they feel sick, or a warm house when you are stuck at home on a cold day. Teach your baby from the beginning to give thanks no matter what happens.

### BABY *Bite*

Our thanks is based on our belief in Christ, faith that isn't dependent on circumstances, no matter how difficult.

## TODDLER *Tips*

Teach your children from
the beginning to give
thanks no matter
what happens.

# TODDLER *Steps*

Toddlers can sign and may even be able to say "thank you"
on their own. It's a great time to begin teaching them to
express gratitude. Teach them to express gratitude by saying
"thank you" to God throughout your day. Thank God for food
at mealtimes, and for a place to sleep at bedtime. You can
also begin teaching your toddler to express gratitude "in
all things" by saying "thank you" to God even in hard times.
Read Bible stories that teach how God helps us in hard times
- stories like Joseph, Moses, or Esther illustrate that God is
always with us. Let your child know that they can say "thank
you" to God no matter what.

# CHAPTER 35

# Respond with Affection

## 📖 MEDITATE

*So does belonging to Christ help you in any way? Does his love comfort you at all? Do you share anything in common because of the Holy Spirit? Has Christ ever been gentle and loving toward you? If any of these things has happened to you, then agree with one another. Have the same love. Be one in spirit and in the way you think and act. By doing this, you will make my joy complete.* – Philippians 2:1-2

Extended passage: Philippians 2:1-18

## ✏️ ANTICIPATE

● Make a list of all the ways God has cared for and shown his love toward you.

_____

_____


● How does God's love and care prompt you to treat others?

_____

_____

After years of avoiding women's ministry (because Drama and Crying), I joined a women's community group and was convicted early on that this group of women would be used by God to help me along my spiritual journey. They walked with me through a difficult pregnancy, when my oldest daughter had surgery to determine if she had cancer, and as I navigated the uncertainty of being a foster parent. This group of women taught me that leaning into hard things makes you stronger. That the work of loving and walking alongside sisters in Christ will bring you so much farther along your spiritual journey than you could ever go alone.

## AFFECTION

Paul writes to the church in Philippi with great affection. He writes of his thankfulness for them, his joy when he thinks of them, and his deep love for them. Then, he urges them to be affectionate - to show love and devotion - to one another. He begins with the premise that as Christ followers, we have enjoyed the privilege of finding joy and comfort and friendship and love in God. And the response that follow is to respond with affection to our brothers and sisters in Christ. Paul challenges them to agree and love and be one in spirit with one another. The Message puts it this way: "be deep spirited friends" (v2).

## WALKING TOGETHER

The mornings I spent with that community group are mornings I will forever cherish. When I got past myself and started being a "deep spirited friend," I learned the value of the unity that Paul instructs us to strive for here. This journey we are on is hard and it takes the affection of deep spirited friends to carry us through. But unless we recognize the gifts we have been given because we belong to Christ, and make the choice to respond to brothers and sisters in Christ with affection, we'll never know the joy found in walking alongside each other along the way.

Photo © Oksana Kuzmina

# BABY *Steps*

Babies respond to and need love and affection. We as parents are tasked with loving our little ones and naturally show affection as we hold, rock, hug, and kiss them. Babies can also begin learning to respond to love and affection from others. Begin teaching them the value of affection among Christ followers by bringing them to church and placing them in proximity to friends and caregivers who will shower them with attention. Bring them to your church's nursery, introduce them to friends or mentors, or have them join you in a community group. Be intentional in the way you show your baby that their faith community is a place where they are loved and cared for.

### BABY *Bite*

This journey we are on is hard sometimes. We struggle and fall and it takes the affection of deep spirited friends to carry us through.

## TODDLER *Tips*

Unless we recognize the gifts we have been given because we belong to Christ, and make the choice to respond to brothers and sisters in Christ with affection, we'll never know the joy found in walking alongside each other along the way.

# TODDLER *Steps*

Toddlers continue to need love and affection and are beginning to form relationships and bonds with adults as well as children. If they attend a class or service with other toddlers at church, encourage them to form relationships with teachers and friends. Greet your child's teachers and their friends' families warmly and pray for them at home. Gather with other families from your faith community outside of church – have informal "play dates," join a community group, or attend family-friendly church events. Talk to your toddler about your faith community and let them know that the people there love and care for each other.

# CHAPTER 36

# Respond with Rest

## MEDITATE

*Therefore, since the promise of entering his rest still stands, let us be careful that none of you be found to have fallen short of it... There remains, then, a Sabbath-rest for the people of God; for anyone who enters God's rest also rests from their works, just as God did from his.*
— Hebrews 4:1, 9-10 (NIV)

Extended passage: Hebrews 4:1-12

## ANTICIPATE

● What activity or practice do you engage in where you lose track of time?

_____

_____

_____

● Describe the difference between rest and busyness.

_____

_____

_____

When my wife started her teaching career, I bought her several children's books to get her library started. One of those books was *Rattletrap Car,* written by Phyllis Root and illustrated by Jill Barton. The book tells the story of a family trying to escape a hot summer day by traveling to the lake to swim. Their old, rattletrap car keeps breaking down along the way and each family member contributes something to help the journey continue. At one point in the story, the engine falls out and the family is stranded on the side of the road, getting hotter and hotter. The baby holds up her three-speed, wind-up, paddlewheel boat and it becomes the engine and the entire family gets an idea. "Go" said the baby. "Go. Go. Go." (Root, P., & Barton, J. (2001). *Rattletrap Car.* Cambridge MA: Candlewick Press.) The boat replaces the engine and they all make it to the lake and back home again.

## GO, GO, GO

The pace of our lives is often "Go. Go. Go." We go all the time. A short trip to the park feels like a lunar landing mission. We load up the minivan with kids and enough baby gear to host a garage sale. Have you ever gone a few months without emptying the diaper bag? Try it sometime. You'll find the evidence of a fast-paced life. The lost sippy cup with weeks old milk curdling inside. A flashlight. The checklist you were missing. Your wallet. It's all there, covered like an archaeological dig with layers of time and busyness.

## REST

In the midst of busyness, we rarely stop and rest. Yet this is exactly what God beckons us to do. In Hebrews we read: "There remains, then, a Sabbath-rest for the people of God; for anyone who enters God's rest also rests from their works, just as God did from his" (Hebrews 4:9-10). When all of the going is gone, there remains a rest for the people of God. God provides rest for you, and the Holy Spirit invites you to press pause and enter into it. We must respond to the Holy Spirit working in our lives by resting in God.

Photo © Andrew Mayovskyy

# BABY *Steps*

Parenting is hard work, busy work, and often demanding work. As parents, we need the Sabbath – the rest it provides, the reminder to turn our focus to God, the time to rest in his presence and his love for us. This week, stop long enough to remember how great the love of God is toward you and how great your love is toward your child. Pick up your child and rest together. Is there anything more wonderful than a baby sleeping in your arms or on your chest? As you stop and rest, verbally express your gratitude to God for the rest you have in him.

## BABY *Bite*

In the midst of busyness, we rarely stop and rest. Yet this is exactly what God requires of us.

## TODDLER *Tips*

Parenting is hard work, busy work, and often demanding work. As parents, we need the Sabbath – the rest it provides, the reminder to turn our focus to God, the time to rest in his presence and his love for us.

## TODDLER *Steps*

As parents, we often find that our schedules and plan revolve around our toddler's rest times. Bedtimes and naptimes for our toddler are a priority, and yet our own rest is often neglected. But we need rest, and in particular, Sabbath rest. We need the time to unwind, to focus on God, and to rest in his presence and love for us. Rest is a rhythm God invites us to revel in. Press pause on the soundtrack of your life. With your toddler, voice gratitude and thanks for the times you get to rest. Practice saying, "Thank you God for rest" before naps or bedtime.

# CHAPTER 37

# Respond with Obedience

## 📖 MEDITATE

*If you love me, keep my commands.* – John 14:15 (NIV)

Extended passage: John 14:15-30

## ✏️ ANTICIPATE

● What tradition do you want to pass on to your children?

_____

_____

● What is the most natural way for you to express love to others?

_____

_____

As parents, we naturally desire to pass on important things, traditions, and beliefs to our children. As I became a parent, I was mindful of one thing I wanted to pass on to my children: a love for Star Wars.

I grew up watching the George Lucas trilogy on VHS tape. I memorized lines and fight scenes. I cheered with the Ewoks when they took down the AT-ST Walker. I shuddered when Admiral Ackbar declared, "It's a trap!" When *Star Wars: Episode I – The Phantom Menace* came out in 1999, I went to see the movie 37 times.

When my children were born I knew I wanted to pass on the tradition of enjoying these classic movies.

## WORDS

Jesus wanted to pass something onto his followers. He makes his desire crystal clear in John 14. In verse one Jesus reassures his disciples, "Let not your hearts be troubled." Jesus expresses care and love for those who followed him and he equips them practically to carry out their commitment. Then in verse 15 Jesus affirmed, "If you love me, keep my commands." These words are the last message Jesus speaks before the greatest act in history commenced, Christ's death for the sin of the world. And in this final speech, Jesus passed along something critical. He clarified what love requires: obedience. And he follows up his statement by introducing the Holy Spirit as the advocate and helper for his people to accomplish it.

## OBEDIENCE

Everyday we must respond to the Holy Spirit in our lives in love toward God and out of that love, obey his Word. Without obedience to God, words of love ring hollow. We must not only acknowledge who God is and what God has done, we must not merely read the words of God in Scripture, we have to follow them with our lives and actions. Only then can our love for God materialize. Our love for God and delight in Jesus must fuel the way we live. As we establish this rhythm in our lives, God will visit upon us in personal, powerful and transforming ways.

Photo © Oksana Kuzmina

# BABY *Steps*

In Jesus' final hours before his arrest and crucifixion, he delivers his final words to his followers. In this passage we discover his promises for those who love him. Pass these promises to your children this week. Set aside a holy moment and pray this blessing over them: "The God who gave his life for you desires to know you and be near to you. May a love for God your Savior fill your life with delight. Out of this love, I pray your life will be defined by obedience to God's Word. From a life of obedience, may you experience intimacy and closeness with God, may your mind and ears and heart be filled with God's words of love and grace."

## BABY *Bite*

As parents, we naturally desire to pass on important things, traditions, and beliefs to our children.

We must not only acknowledge who God is and what God has done, we must not merely read the words of God in Scripture, we have to follow them with our lives and actions. Only then can our love for God materialize.

# TODDLER *Steps*

The promises found in John 14 were delivered just before Jesus' arrest and crucifixion. They were among his final words spoken to those who loved him. Pass these promises to your children this week. Set aside a holy moment and pray this blessing over them: "My son/daughter, I love you so much. Words are difficult to express the great love I have for you, but God's love for you is even bigger. And your life could explode with love back to God for all he has done for you. Through your love for God, may you desire to listen to his words and follow his directions. Out of your obedience, may you see God at work around you always."

# CHAPTER 38

# Respond with Faith

## 📖 MEDITATE

*"Faith is being sure of what we hope for. It is being sure of what we do not see."* – Hebrews 11:1

Extended passage: Hebrews 11:1-2

## ✏️ ANTICIPATE

● What things do you wish you knew about the future that would help you be a better parent today?

_____

_____

_____

● What hopes and dreams do you have for your child's future?

_____

_____

_____

My first and last babies have a lot of similarities, but my experiences in caring for them in those hazy sleep-deprived days of babyhood are opposite extremes. With Isabel (my first), I was anxious and awkward and always eager to move through the current stage, which always dragged along slowly, hoping the next one would be easier. With Josie (my last), I am more calm and comfortable and I take the time to cherish each stage, which seem to pass too quickly.

## THE DIFFERENCE

Between my first and last babies, I spent a decade learning, gaining confidence and perspective, becoming a mama more sure of herself and less unsure of how things would work out. I can enjoy Josie even on hard days, because I know that in a blink she'll be a lovely, amazing, more grown up version of her baby self – just like her big sister Isabel. With Isabel, I hoped for so many things – that she would know I loved her, that she would grow to be strong and confident, that she would love Jesus and know his love for her. Now that I have seen some of those things blossoming in her heart and her actions, I am a little more sure of what I hoped for. I look at her, and I feel more sure of myself and of God at work in me as I parent Josie.

## FAITH IS THE FOUNDATION

Hebrews 11 urges us to have something that I struggled with in my early days of parenting: faith. Being sure of what I hoped for *even when it was too far off for me to see.* Our faith in God is what we stand on. It's the only thing that can't be shaken, the very thing that gives our life meaning. Faith gives us something to hold onto when **we can't** see beyond the next turn in the road. While parenting is hard work, it is also holy work. He already has a perfect plan for our child's future, and this passage encourages us that when we can't see what's ahead, when we are unsure of our way, we respond in faith, sure of what we hope for and cannot yet see.

Photo © Marlon Lopez MMG1 Design

163

# BABY *Steps*

Babies come into this world full of potential. As parents, we are filled with hopes and dreams for their future that seem limitless. Take time this week to pray about your baby's future, asking God to place a few things on your heart that you hope for as you consider your baby's future. What do you want them to know and feel? How do you want them to respond to God? Write these things down and take time to pray that God will give you faith to be sure of the things that you hope for. Dedicate your hopes for your child to God; hold your baby and pray, having faith that God has a plan for their future.

## BABY *Bite*

Our faith in God is what we stand on. It's the only thing that can't be shaken, the very thing that gives our life meaning.

## TODDLER *Tips*

While parenting is hard
work, it is also holy work.

## TODDLER *Steps*

As our babies grow into toddlers, we see more of their personalities and gifts emerge. Our hopes and dreams for them are often prompted by their budding interests - they love to fix things and we see a future engineer. They are caring and kind and we see a future doctor. Take time this week to pray about your toddler's future, asking God to show you how the gifts he created them with are part of his plan for their future. Write down a few things that you feel God placing on your heart as you consider and hope for your toddler's future. Pray over this list, asking God to give you faith to be sure of what you hope for. Then show it to your toddler and pray together, dedicating your hopes for your child to God, having faith that he has a plan for their future.

# CHAPTER 39

# Respond with Compassion

## MEDITATE

*Therefore, as God's chosen people, holy and dearly loved, clothe yourselves with compassion, kindness, humility, gentleness and patience. Bear with each other and forgive one another if any of you has a grievance against someone. Forgive as the Lord forgave you.*
— Colossians 3:12-13 (NIV)

Extended passage: Colossians 3:1-17

## ANTICIPATE

● Describe the outfit you took your child home from the hospital in.

_____

_____

_____

● What is your favorite outfit?

_____

_____

God gave me three daughters. *Three. Daughters.*

Having three daughters in my house is often completely baffling for me. I remember actually spending time thinking through the outfit each of our children would wear home from the hospital. I don't know why - I spend as little time as possible thinking about clothes and would prefer to wear the exact same outfit every day. But babies have lots and lots of clothes. I remember seeing all of the clothes stack up after we had our first child, then our second child. Bins of clothes lined our basement. Bins for different seasons and sizes. So. Many. Clothes.

## CLOTHE YOURSELVES

Much to my dismay, the Bible talks about clothing often. Different biblical characters are identified by their clothing. Adam and Eve wearing the clothes God made for them after they sinned in the Garden of Eden. Joseph and the coat of many colors. The holy garments of the priests and Levites. John the Baptist and his clothing of camel's hair. But the apostle Paul speaks of clothing in a unique way - he instructs the people of God, those who have put their faith and trust in Jesus, to clothe themselves not with a new set of robes but a new set of characteristics.

## WITH COMPASSION

In Colossians 3 Paul charges, "clothe yourselves with compassion, kindness, humility, gentleness and patience." Paul makes this claim because of what Christ accomplished for us. We are able to clothe ourselves with compassion and kindness because through Christ's redemptive work on the cross, we are made new. We have been made new. So we can discard the old outfits we once wore of unforgiveness, hard heartedness, anger, pride, harshness, judgment, and impatience and in turn, embrace compassion.

Sounds like a good deal to me.

# BABY *Steps*

Babies give us plenty of opportunities to practice compassion. Compassion means "to suffer with." Here in Colossians and throughout the Bible, compassion is often tied to or mentioned alongside forgiveness. As parents, we need forgiveness because we do not always act as God commands toward our children. We can create an environment where we embrace compassion by modeling what it means to repent and ask for forgiveness when we need it. As you dress your child this week, think of Colossians 3. I know it can be tedious to get a baby ready – their bodies often turn into gelatin or into a statue when getting dressed. If they cry or become upset, have compassion on them. Fight the urge to rush and help them get through it. If you do become frustrated or impatient, repent and ask for forgiveness.

## BABY *Bite*

We are able to clothe ourselves with compassion and kindness because through Christ's redemptive work on the cross, we are made new.

## TODDLER *Tips*

As parents, we need forgiveness because we do not always act as God commands toward our children. We can create an environment where we embrace compassion by modeling what it means to repent and ask for forgiveness when we need it.

# TODDLER *Steps*

Because toddlers are still in a developmental stage where they are completely focused on themselves, understanding when they have made a mistake can be difficult. They are just learning to understand that other people have feelings, and are still focused on their own feelings. Compassion, or "suffering with" is often mentioned alongside forgiveness in the Bible. As parents, we need forgiveness because we often struggle to treat our children the way God commands us to. We can create a home that embraces compassion by modeling repentance, asking forgiveness when we need it. You can illustrate compassion to them by modeling what it looks like to say you're sorry. If you accidentally run into your toddler (this happens at our house all the time) or forget to follow through on something, show your toddler what it looks like to ask for forgiveness.

# Model Prayer

## MEDITATE

*Rejoice always, pray continually, give thanks in all circumstances; for this is God's will for you in Christ Jesus.* – 1 Thessalonians 5:16-18 (NIV)

Extended passage: 1 Thessalonians 5:12-28

## ANTICIPATE

● What do you pray about?

_____

_____

_____

● What keeps you from praying or talking to God freely?

_____

_____

_____

From the time my daughter Isabel learned the words and was able to string them together, she told me, "My tummy hurts." Her stomach hurt all the time. Every day and every night. As a little girl, she would keel over and grab her stomach. Her face would wince from the stinging discomfort. Other times she would wake up screaming in the middle of the night. There are few things more difficult than watching your child in pain, especially pain you can do nothing about.

## DOCTORS

We took Isabel to so many doctors, I cannot even remember the number. Specialists of every kind examined Isabel. After every test, at every hospital, with every specialist we could meet with, nothing was conclusive. Doctors did not know what to do except prescribe pain medication. They told me my daughter would be taking these pills every day of her life.

## PRAYER

At that time, a wise friend took me aside to share Paul's final instructions in 1 Thessalonians. At the end of the apostle's letter to the church he writes, "Rejoice always, pray continually, give thanks in all circumstances; for this is God's will for you in Christ Jesus." I struggled with this diagnosis even more than the doctors. Rejoice? Pray? Give thanks? I did not know what else I could do, so I gave in. I prayed over my daughter. With undiagnosed pain attacking Isabel's body daily, I prayed with my wife, parents, friends, coworkers. I met with my pastor and church leaders to ask for prayer. Isabel had an army of people on their knees praying for years. This was no easy journey and it still brings tears to my eyes. But when we walk difficult roads with God, he leads us to beautiful places. We do not want to pray or rejoice or give thanks on these roads, but that's what moves us forward. Eventually, God healed Isabel. The pain was removed completely and today she lives out Paul's words in 1 Thessalonians better than anyone I know.

Photo © John Wollwerth

# BABY Steps

All babies fall into a routine - it doesn't always follow a clock, but your baby will regularly eat, sleep, and be awake. Paul's words in 1 Thessalonians to pray continually, over and over again, can feel overwhelming as you try to fit in one more thing into your erratic daily routine. Prayer wasn't intended to be just "one more thing." It is The Thing that bubbles up into delight, for as we spend time talking to God, we learn to delight in him. We learn to rejoice and give thanks. This week, make your prayers a continual conversation with God. In all aspects of your baby's routine, keep the conversation going. Use their rhythms as a prompt to have ongoing communication with God. Voice your thoughts to God. Confess sin to God. Honor God for who he is and what he has done. If you are facing a tough situation, do not give up praying. Enlist others to join your dedicated prayer efforts.

BABY Bite

As we spend time talking to God, we learn to delight in him. We learn to rejoice and give thanks.

## TODDLER *Tips*

Let the daily rhythms of your life prompt simple and honest prayers to God

# TODDLER *Steps*

Toddlers may fall into a more predictable routine, but still our days are filled with a longer to do list than we can ever check off. Paul's instructions to pray continually, to speak to God over and over, can feel like one more thing on that insurmountable to do list. But this was never God's plan. Prayer is intended to bring us joy. As we spend time talking to God, we learn to delight in him. Through continued communion, we are able to rejoice and give thanks. This week, parent your toddler with continuous prayer and invitations for them to pray with you. Let your regular rhythms prompt simple and honest prayers. Before mealtimes or reading a Bible story, ask them, "Will you pray with me?" If you need prayer, extend an invitation to your child, "Will you pray for me?" If your toddler expresses a need, answer them with "Let's pray about that together." Encourage them to start the prayer and you follow.

# CHAPTER 41

# Model Bible Reading

## 📖 MEDITATE

*These commandments that I give you today are to be on your hearts. Impress them on your children. Talk about them when you sit at home and when you walk along the road, when you lie down and when you get up.* – Deuteronomy 6:6-7 (NIV)

Extended passage: Deuteronomy 6:4-9

## ✏️ ANTICIPATE

● What is something you love doing?

_____

_____

● What is something that requires consistent effort for you to do?

_____

_____

Most parents love or despise bath time. Bath time can be something they look forward to or a tiring chore. I love the bath time ritual. I have taken care of bath time for all our kids. Turning a room in your house into a mini swimming pool and loading a tub with bubbles seems like one of the most imaginative things you can do for your child. Plus, they end up smelling a lot better when you're finished. But here's the thing. When I am traveling, mom has to handle bath time and she sits on the other side of the spectrum. At the end of a long day, bath time is tough.

## DELIGHT AND DISCIPLINE

There is a significant difference between delight and discipline. Think about something you truly delight in - you enjoy it, it gives you energy, and you look forward to it. For some parents this might include going on vacation, cooking, reading a book, or sports activity. I delight in spending time with my family (confession: I also delight in eating ice cream). Now think about something requiring discipline for you. You have to schedule it. You may even put it off. It is a chore. What do you need discipline to do?

## WHEN YOU...

Moses, who wrote the book of Deuteronomy, delighted in the law. He had the incredible privilege of hearing God dictate the 10 Commandments. Moses witnessed God accomplish supernatural miracles. And in Deuteronomy 6, he inspires families to begin integrating the words of God into their daily rhythm: when you sit at home, when you walk along the road, when you lie down and when you get up. When we consider showing our children what it looks like to be a regular Bible reader, we must determine whether or not this rhythm will be a discipline or a delight. And if we follow the pattern of Deuteronomy 6, we will find our entire family delighting in God's Word each day.

Photo © fotorawin

# BABY *Steps*

This week, read the Bible. Don't try to finish the whole thing, just follow a simple plan to read a little every day. If you have struggled to read the Bible in the past, try using a different translation. Work to find a translation that is easy for you to read. Open the Bible in front of your infant and encourage them to touch the pages. Pray you will begin to savor God's words and ask God to grow a love for the Scripture in your child.

## BABY *Bite*

When we consider showing our children what it looks like to be a regular Bible reader, we must determine whether or not this rhythm will be a discipline or a delight.

As you read the Bible
to your children, read it
dynamically and
with feeling.

# TODDLER *Steps*

This week, read the Bible together. Share the verses you
are reading or utilize a Bible storybook with your toddler.
Just as it is important for you to find a version of the Bible
that helps you grow in delight, find a Bible storybook
your child loves to look at and listen to. Encourage your
toddler to sit in your lap as you read. Flipping pages is a
vital pre-reading skill, so involve your toddler as you move
through the story. As you read the Bible to your toddler,
read it dynamically and with feeling. Let them interact with
the pictures and respond to the story.

# CHAPTER 42

# Model Worship

## 📖 MEDITATE

*"Worship the LORD with gladness. Come to him with songs of joy."*

– Psalm 100:2

Extended passage: Psalm 100

## ✏️ ANTICIPATE

● How do you express worship to God?

_____

_____

_____

● What do you enjoy most about worship?

_____

_____

_____

My youngest daughter, Josie, loves music. She is too young to understand or sing along, but the sound of music playing fills her with joy. When I'm having a rough day, I often turn on worship music and while I don't express joy in the same way, I do find that something about the rhythms and melodies reaches deep in my soul and helps me connect with my Creator. When I'm having a good day, I often turn on worship music as well, and I find that it helps me remember that the things that fill my heart with joy are gifts from my heavenly Father.

## PSALMS OF WORSHIP

Throughout Psalms, we read songs of worship that come from hearts that are heavy with sorrow on one page and overflowing with praise the next. David pens some of Israel's most famous worship songs while running for his life. When he is lonely, or hurt, or weary, he responds with worship. Other psalms David writes in celebration of victory. When he is thankful, or triumphant, or vindicated, he responds with worship. There are 150 Psalms in the Bible, written by different psalmists inspired by trials and triumphs who respond to God in worship, leading the people of Israel to do the same. Centuries later, their worship response stands as a model for us, a reminder that we, too, can respond and lead out in worship.

## IN JOY AND SORROW

Psalm 100 is a psalm filled with joy. It prompts us to recognize that our joy can be used to worship God. When you have joyful days, model for your child that worship is the appropriate response. But other psalms are filled with sorrow. They prompt us to share our burdens with a Father who loves us, and then worship him because he is our strength. When you have sorrowful days, model for your child that worship is the appropriate response. We will have good days and bad and how we respond teaches our children how they should respond, as well. Modeling worship gives our children a way to connect with God, no matter what is happening around them.

Photo © Darren Liby

# BABY *Steps*

Babies love music, and will often bounce, sway, or clap as they become more coordinated. Even newborns are often soothed or stimulated by music, depending on the type of music and their unique tastes. (My oldest daughter preferred the Blues during middle of the night cry sessions). This week, choose a worship song that you can sing when you are joyful, and another worship song that you can sing when you are sorrowful, illustrating that you can always worship God, no matter what. These can be hymns, modern day worship songs, or even Psalms from Scripture. Hold or sit near your baby as you sing these songs throughout the week, modeling worship in good times and bad.

## BABY *Bite*

When you have joyful days, model for your child that worship is the appropriate response.

## TODDLER *Tips*

We will have good days and bad and how we respond teaches our children how they should respond, as well. Modeling worship gives our children a way to connect with God, no matter what is happening around them.

# TODDLER *Steps*

Toddlers love music as well, and are learning that they can participate with singing, dancing, or playing music. Many toddlers have favorite songs and will request them over and over. This week, choose worship songs that you can sing on good days and bad. Look for a couple of songs with simple melodies and lyrics that your toddler could sing with you. They can be adult songs or songs written for children. Then sing these songs with your toddler throughout the week, illustrating that worship connects us to God, in good times and bad. Explain that this song helps you worship or show your love for God when you feel sad or happy. Let them know that we can always worship God, no matter what happens.

# CHAPTER 43

# Model Celebration

## MEDITATE

*"They celebrate your great goodness. They sing for joy about your holy acts."* – Psalm 145:7

Extended passage: Psalm 145

## ANTICIPATE

● What are some of your favorite celebrations?

_____
_____

● How will you (or did you) celebrate your child's first birthday?

_____
_____
_____

First birthdays are always momentous occasions. That first year feels a bit like a marathon – a long distance event filled with milestones big and small – and reaching the finish line seems like a major accomplishment for both parent and child. Celebrating my son Zion's first birthday was especially meaningful for me because his birth was an answer to so many desperate prayers. When we reached that first year milestone, we threw a big celebration. I sat with my son, surrounded with loved ones who had prayed us through a difficult season and then celebrated and loved our son as the miraculous gift that he is. The celebration was a reminder that God carried us through a difficult time and blessed us beyond what we could have imagined.

## THE FEASTS

The Old Testament and New are filled with instructions that God gave to his people to gather together and celebrate the good things God had done. In addition to the Sabbath, the Israelites gathered together to celebrate seven feasts each year. These feasts prompted God's people to celebrate stories of God's goodness, be reminded of his faithfulness, teach the next generation how to worship, and look forward with hope to a time when God's covenant would be fulfilled in the coming Messiah.

## TRADITION OF CELEBRATION

While most of us don't celebrate the traditional Jewish feasts, it is important that we model for our children what it means to celebrate who God is and what he has done. As parents, moving forward in the journey means taking moments to celebrate how far God has brought us. Gathering to worship God for his goodness and praising him for his mighty acts keep us focused on our dependence on God to guide us, and provides a meaningful way to pass on our faith to the next generation. It keeps God central in our journey, and orients us so that we are reminded of how far we've come, and prompted to keep following as God guides us forward.

Photo © Amelia Fox

# BABY *Steps*

Celebrations are a natural part of a baby's routine. We clap and cheer each time our baby learns a new skill and they quickly learn to join in the celebration. Begin incorporating celebrations that commemorate who God is and what he has done. Look through your calendar and mark days that you will intentionally celebrate God's goodness and holy acts. You may want to simply fold these into your regular celebrations – considering how you could place a greater focus on celebrating God during special days like holidays or birthdays. As you gather with family and friends, praise God for what he has done in your lives. You could also read about and celebrate the feasts outlined in the Old Testament, incorporating some of those traditions while making them your own. Model celebration for your baby so they grow to see it as a natural part of their journey.

## BABY *Bite*

It is important for parents to model for our children what it means to celebrate who God is and what he has done.

TODDLER *Tips*

Look through your calendar
and mark days that you will
intentionally celebrate God's
goodness and holy acts.

# TODDLER *Steps*

Toddlers have likely experienced formal and informal celebrations and can begin being a more active participant in these special occasions. If you haven't already, look through your calendar and mark days that you will intentionally celebrate God's goodness and holy acts. Whether you decide to fold these celebrations into your holiday gatherings and traditions, incorporate biblical feasts outlined in the Old Testament into your family calendar, or create new celebrations of your own, model God-focused celebration for your toddler so it will become a familiar and anticipated part of their journey.

# CHAPTER 44

# Model Service

## MEDITATE

*"My brothers and sisters, you were chosen to be free. But don't use your freedom as an excuse to live under the power of sin. Instead, serve one another in love."* – Galatians 5:13

Extended passage: Galatians 5

## ANTICIPATE

● What does it mean to "serve others?"

_____

_____

_____

● In what ways do you enjoy serving others? In what ways are you tempted to resent it?

_____

_____

_____

Right now, I am busy with four children, a puppy, and a child we are hosting through Safe Families. I love my life as much as I'm exhausted by it. Sometimes I feel like I'm cruising through and other times I have more plates to spin than energy to spin them. It's in those moments that I sometimes feel like I have the right to nurse a grudge, or strike out at whoever is closest.

## COUNTER-CULTURE

Our culture encourages us to look out for #1. But God is always calling us to live counter-culturally and in Galatians we read that we have freedom from sin, not to sin. Paul tells us that instead of using our freedom as an excuse to continue sinning, we should serve one another in love. In this season, I am plearning that my To Do list is really a list of serving opportunities. And as I serve my family, my children big and small are seeing what it means to serve one another. The hard part is to do it in love. The next step, as I model serving in love, is to give my children plenty of opportunities to follow my lead. If I do everything for them and call it "serving in love," I rob them of the opportunity to serve each other. In our home we ask the question, "what needs to be done?" I carry Josie on my hip and she watches as I tidy counters and help with homework. My three-year-old son Zion knows his big sisters will help when he asks, and he is learning to do the same. It's a work in progress, and some days our sin natures win. But when I get off track, God is always faithful to restore me and I am free to try again

## SETTING THE EXAMPLE

Serving in love is hard work. Our example is Jesus, who served us selflessly and made the ultimate sacrifice for us when we didn't deserve it, while we were still sinners. As parents, we have the opportunity day in and day out to model serving for our children, praying that one day they will grow to serve in love as well.

Photo © Tatyana Vyc

# BABY *Steps*

Our babies begin watching us on the day they are born, learning by seeing what we do long before they are able to imitate us. You can model serving in love for your baby as you serve them and others on a daily basis. Ask God to help you see even the most mundane tasks – changing diapers, midnight feedings, doing laundry – as opportunities to serve in love. As you care for your baby, tell them you love them. Let them learn from your example that serving is a way to show love to one another.

## BABY *Bite*

It's the human condition to look out for #1. In fact, our culture would support and even encourage it. But God is always calling us to live counter-culturally.

## TODDLER *Tips*

Serving in love is hard work.
Our example is Jesus, who
served us selflessly and
made the ultimate sacrifice
for us when we didn't
deserve it, while we were
still sinners.

# TODDLER *Steps*

Toddlers love "helping" and copying what their parents
do around the house. As you go about your everyday
tasks of cooking, cleaning, and caring for your toddler,
model serving in love by telling your child you love them.
Invite your toddler to help - give them napkins to set on
the table, have them help put away their toys, show them
how to put their dirty clothes in the laundry basket. As
they do, thank them for serving others. Set an example of
serving in love, then invite them to follow your lead.

# CHAPTER 45

# Model Solitude

 **MEDITATE**

*But when you pray, go into your room, close the door and pray to your Father, who is unseen. Then your Father, who sees what is done in secret, will reward you.* – Matthew 6:6 (NIV)

Extended passage: Matthew 6:5-14

 **ANTICIPATE**

● When do you get the opportunity to pull away and spend time alone?

_____

_____

_____

● Do you gain energy from being with people or being by yourself?

_____

_____

_____

Air travel with a baby is industrial strength parenting. You can never pack enough supplies for a baby on a plane. You gather everything possible. Bottles, blankets, toys, snacks, diapers, wipes, changing pad, medicine in case they get sick, back-up clothing in case of an accident, a second set of clothing for you in case of an accident, and one thousand other things. Airports are not meant for infants. In fact, when you travel on a plane with an infant, people generally respond negatively.

## THE NOTE

I came across a news story about parents traveling with a 12 month old. In order to combat the unfavorable sentiment most people have when they encounter a baby, the parents packed a note and some treats for the people sitting around them. The note read: "Hi Stranger! My name is Madeline. I will be 1 on December 17th and this is my first flight. I'll try to be on my best behavior, but I'd like to apologize in advance if I lose my cool, get scared or my ears hurt. My mom and dad packed you this goodie bag with a few treats. There are also earplugs in case my first public serenade isn't as enjoyable to you as it is to my mom and dad. Have a great flight!" I do not recommend ever doing this. You have to pack enough for the whole plane.

## UP AND AWAY

In days gone by, a plane was a place you could remain totally disconnected from the world around you, the roles you play, your email inbox, phone calls and text messages. Now you can do anything on a plane you can do at your desk. (I wrote this devotional on a plane.) Jesus tells his followers to do something counter cultural, both by ancient and modern standards. Jesus commands them to pull away from the world around them and talk to God privately. There is something important about this practice of solitude. When you remove yourself from the world around you, you gain perspective unavailable in our always on, always available culture.

Photo © AlohaHawaii

# BABY *Steps*

One of the greatest practices to model solitude for your family is to regularly power off your phone. Spend time each day with your device (phone, tablet, or laptop) powered off. This week, intentionally leave your phone in a drawer for extended periods of time. Instead of using your phone to capture videos and pictures, lean on your eyes and memory to capture them instead. Find time to pull away from the busy pace together. Create an environment of solitude. Keep the lights down low and remove distractions so you can focus on being present with your child.

## BABY *Bite*

There is something important about this practice of solitude. When you remove yourself from the world around you, you gain perspective unavailable in our always on, always available culture.

## TODDLER *Tips*

One of the greatest practices to model solitude for your family is to regularly power off your phone.

# TODDLER *Steps*

One of the unique things about parenting a toddler is naptime allows for the practice of solitude. You can practice solitude together during this part of the daily routine. As you prepare for naptime this week, combine reading a Bible story and praying with your little one. If your toddler is anxious before nap, let them know they can still talk to God during this time. Practice God conversations with them. Have your child repeat simple phrases after you say them like, "Hi, God." "I love you, God." "Good night, God."

# CHAPTER 46

# Model Honor

## MEDITATE

*Do you not know that your bodies are temples of the Holy Spirit, who is in you, whom you have received from God? You are not your own; you were bought at a price. Therefore honor God with your bodies.*

– 1 Corinthians 6:19-20 (NIV)

Extended passage: 1 Corinthians 6:12-20

## ANTICIPATE

● In the hospital, how often did nurses offer to take care of your baby for you?

_____

_____

_____

● What are some of the ways you enjoy giving God praise?

_____

_____

All four of my children were born in hospitals across southern Wisconsin and Northern Illinois. My first child was born 10 years, 10 months, and 11 days before my fourth child. When I take a beat to think about it, this is quite the span. Yet, the experience in the hospital was virtually the same over the decade span. Hours of delivery, recovery, and then trying to sleep in between nurses coming in every couple hours to check vitals and update charts. The biggest difference over the ten years was how often the nurses took care of the baby for us.

## BELONGING

When our first baby was born, the nurses offered to take the baby regularly. It was so wonderful I did not want to leave the hospital. I had no idea what I was doing! How could they let me leave and take care of this child? How would we survive without the nurses? When our fourth baby was born, the nurses never took the baby out of our room. I couldn't wait to leave the hospital and go home. In all four cases, I came to the realization when it was finally time to come home from the hospital, the babies strapped into their carseats were mine. No one else could care for these children. Not nurses or doctors or practitioners. These children belonged to me.

## HONOR GOD

In 1 Corinthians, Paul writes about ownership by discussing honor. Honor is not about what we bring to God, it is about recognizing the fact we belong to God alone. Honor allows us to rightly prioritize who God is and what God has done for us because we understand everything we are belongs to God and everything we have comes from his hand. Throughout the Bible we read passages like Psalm 95:6-7, 1 Timothy 2:8, and Psalm 63:4 challenging us to use our bodies to honor God and give him praise. Sometimes it might be a struggle to know how best to honor God, but these verses give us options. We can bow, kneel, and lift up our hands and show God the honor he deserves.

Photo © Oleksiy Avtomonov

# BABY *Steps*

This week, sing a song of praise with your infant. Teach them to lift their hands as you sing. If they are too little, lift your baby's hands for them. Around 9 months, your baby will begin to clap their hands. Take time to model clapping. Put your hands on your baby's and clap together as you listen to songs giving God honor.

## BABY *Bite*

Honor is not about what we bring to God, it is about recognizing the fact we belong to God alone.

## TODDLER *Tips*

The position of the soul follows the position of the body. When was the last time you used your body to honor God?

# TODDLER *Steps*

Toddlers can be challenged even more to use their body to give God praise and honor. Take time to learn a song with motions in it. Talk to your church and find out what songs your toddler sings. Your child may actually be the one to challenge you, because they know the song and have learned the actions. Honor God together!

# Model the Sabbath

## MEDITATE

*Remember the Sabbath day by keeping it holy. Six days you shall labor and do all your work, but the seventh day is a sabbath to the LORD your God.* – Exodus 20:8-10 (NIV)

Extended passage: Exodus 20:1-21

## ANTICIPATE

● How do you pause and rest in the midst of a busy schedule?

_____

_____

_____

● What do you enjoy doing?

_____

_____

_____

What would you do with four hours with no kids? I had the chance to plan a four-hour vacation once, thanks to grandparents offering to take over for us. This came after a long season of kid-only living. Getting a break was simply not an option. So my plan was going to be perfect – I was trying to pack months of date nights into the ultimate night to remember: a romantic dinner at a fancy restaurant, going to see a movie without cartoon characters, stopping at the park for a long walk, grabbing dessert and coffee at our favorite spot. Maybe somewhere along the way we would stop by a church to renew our vows and release a flock of doves before coming home. In four hours we would do all of the things. It was all there. We were grateful for the gift of time away and knew we could make the most of it.

## SURPRISE

The day came and the grandparents picked up the kids. How do you think we spent the next few hours?

We took a nap.

Before we left the house, we went upstairs to grab something and thought we would just rest for a few minutes. We were so exhausted, so weary, we crashed. All dressed up, we simply fell asleep until the doorbell rang four hours later. It was one of those naps when you wake up, you forget where you are or what day it is. No dinner. No romantic walk. No doves. Just rest.

## SABBATH

God's plan for your life includes work. But it also includes rest. God saw rest as so essential to the rhythm of life that he paused after creation to rest on the seventh day. When God laid out his commands to the people of Israel he made clear, work six days and then rest. This is Sabbath.

Most families do not practice Sabbath. We run hard 24/7. But it is our responsibility to obey God and model rest to our children. When we rest we affirm to ourselves, our kids, and our world – we trust God. The world can continue without me working.

Photo © Oksana Kuzmina

# BABY *Steps*

During Sabbath, take time to enjoy your infant. Take the time without your phone or laptop to distract you and just enjoy them. The world will continue without your checking email or Facebook. Delight in your child as God delights in you. Hold them close. As you model this rest and delight, your infant will see the joy and love reflect in your eyes and face and know they are worth being loved and cared for.

## BABY *Bite*

God's plan for your life includes work. But it also includes rest. God saw rest as so essential to the rhythm of life that he paused after creation to rest on the seventh day.

## TODDLER *Tips*

When we rest we affirm to ourselves, our kids, and our world – we trust God. The world can continue without our work.

# TODDLER *Steps*

During Sabbath, reinforce an intentionally slow pace with your toddler. Simply slow down. Walk slower, take time to breathe deeply, resist the urge to rush, try to eat your meals slowly. Fight the urge to fill your Sabbath with a to do list. Find something you enjoy doing with your toddler and take the time to have fun together. Share how God commanded his people to rest and truly set the day apart.

# CHAPTER 48

# Model Giving

## MEDITATE

*"Each of you should give what you have decided in your heart to give, not reluctantly or under compulsion, for God loves a cheerful giver."*
- 2 Corinthians 9:7 (NIV)

Extended passage: 2 Corinthians 9

## ANTICIPATE

● Do you consider yourself a cheerful giver?

_____

_____

● What holds you back from being more generous?

_____

_____

_____

When my children were small and we were adjusting to less income and all the increased costs that come with having a growing family, I struggled with being a cheerful or even a faithful giver. There was a point when bills were piling up, our savings had dwindled, and for the first time, we looked at our finances through the lens of God's Word. The Bible outlines a unique perspective on money and possessions, reminding us that everything we have is a gift from God. My job is to be a wise steward of those things, and to manage my blessings so that I can use them to bless others. With this fresh perspective, we made a commitment to be cheerful givers, not tithing out of obligation, but because we wanted to be faithful to return back to God a portion of what he had entrusted us with.

## REWARD

In the months that followed our budget makeover, we saw drastic changes in our financial situation. We had setbacks along the way, but as we were faithful to manage our money in ways that aligned with God's Word, we began to reap the rewards of being disciplined and wise stewards. More importantly, we learned to be cheerful givers. We brought our tithe reluctantly at first, but soon obedience did the work of changing our hearts, and we began to look forward to sharing our blessings. When we were able to give above and beyond our "tithe," blessing a friend or responding to a crisis, we felt true joy.

## CHEERFUL GIVERS

Thankfully, we learned to be cheerful givers while our children were small, in large part because our parents modeled it for us. I don't know that we would have made those crucial changes to the way we managed our money had our parents not set the example, and I know that we would have suffered financially and spiritually as a result. Now we get to set the example for our children, so they learn from a young age what it means to be a cheerful giver.

Photo © chrisbrignell

# BABY *Steps*

Having a baby is costly, and often requires a complete budget overhaul. While it's tempting to consider "giving" as an optional expense, God's Word commands Christ followers to give regularly, through tithes and offerings. This can be challenging, but God gives us commands for our own good, and we obey because we trust him. Commit to setting an example right from the start, modeling giving for your baby. Teach them to be a cheerful giver before they even understand it, so they grow to see God as Provider.

## BABY *Bite*

When we are faithful with the things God entrusts us with, and when we are generous in how we share them with others, he often entrusts us with more.

TODDLER *Tips*

Commit to setting an example right from the start, modeling giving for your children.

# TODDLER *Steps*

Toddlers love to imitate their parents, and are beginning to understand joy in giving as well as receiving. Begin teaching your toddler that the things you have - money, food, possessions - are blessings from God. Teach them that God is their Provider. Model sharing those blessings with others, inviting loved ones over for a meal or sharing outgrown clothes and toys with a friend or charity. Have your toddler bring coins or dollar bills to place in the offering at church - make it a fun and exciting celebration so your toddler learns at a young age what it means to be a cheerful giver.

# CHAPTER 49

# Model the Great Commission

## MEDITATE

*He said to them, "Go into all the world and preach the gospel to all creation."* – Mark 16:15 (NIV)

Extended passage: Mark 16:9-20

## ANTICIPATE

● What significant place from your childhood would you like to take your children?

_____

_____

● What childhood story do you remember that most of your family has forgotten?

_____

_____

I will never forget what it felt like when my parents dropped me off at college and I walked up to the fifth floor of my dormitory in downtown Minneapolis. The fact I was in a new city, without a friend in the building, looking at a large shrine set up by my roommate to honor the Green Bay Packers made me feel completely outside of my comfort zone. Not only because I'm the opposite of a Packer fan, but also because I felt so disconnected from everything I was familiar with. I met up with my parents with the weight of fear on my shoulders and heart. I was starting to rethink the whole college thing. But my dad walked up to me and, looking me straight in the eye, revealed, "Matt, you can do this. You can do this. And if you can't, I'll be there."

So I did it.

## THE MISSION

Jesus inspired his disciples with a final challenge before he ascended to heaven. "Go and preach." Jesus' followers had a mission and a message. Imagine what they must have felt hearing those words. All throughout the first four books of the New Testament, we do not read about any of disciples preaching. We do not hear many of their words outside of questions they asked Jesus. Instead, the historical account we have of Jesus and his followers primarily contains words Jesus spoke, messages Jesus taught, places Jesus led his disciples to. Now all of that changed instantly with three words. Go and preach.

## YOUR MISSION

Moms and dads, we share this mission. Your mission as a parent is to go and share The Story. As a follower of Jesus, you have the privilege of carrying the message of Jesus' love and redemption to others. This is a radical responsibility. You might feel hesitant or anxious to open your mouth and share what God has accomplished in Jesus. You might wonder, what will people think? How will they respond? But don't be distracted. Our mission is not to control the responses of others to who God is and what God has done, it is simply to go and to tell.

Photo © Africa Studio

# BABY *Steps*

The Greek word for Gospel is translated "good news." This is the story we are given to share with our children. It's good news! This week, tell your baby "I have good news. Jesus loves you." Repeat this phrase each day with joy.

## BABY *Bite*

As a follower of Jesus, you have the privilege of carrying the message of Jesus' love and redemption to others. This is a radical responsibility.

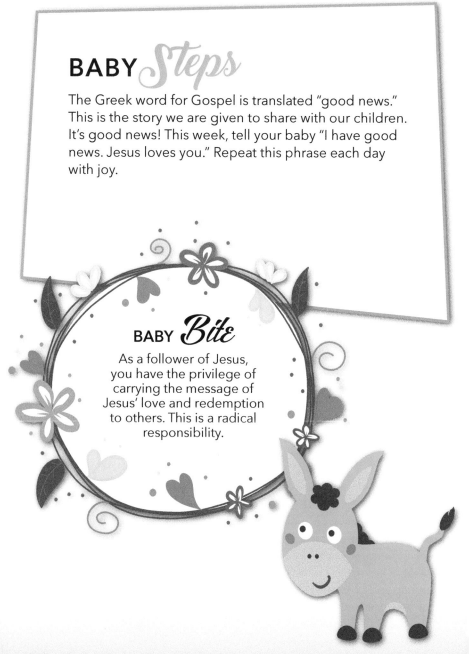

## TODDLER *Tips*

Our mission is not to control the responses of others to who God is and what God has done, it is simply to go and to tell.

# TODDLER *Steps*

This week, teach your toddler to say "I have good news, Jesus loves you." Encourage them to share their good news with others. Start with people they are familiar with like friends or grandparents. See how many people you can share the good news with together.

# CHAPTER 50

# Model Faith Community

## 📖 MEDITATE

*"And let us consider how we may spur one another on toward love and good deeds, not giving up meeting together, as some are in the habit of doing, but encouraging one another..."* – Hebrews 10:24-25 (NIV)

Extended passage: Hebrews 10:19-39

## ✏️ ANTICIPATE

● What do you enjoy about your church or faith community?

_____

_____

_____

● How has your faith community supported or encouraged you?

_____

_____

_____

A few days after my son Zion was born, we moved into a new (to us) home. We spent his first night at home surrounded by boxes piled high, our last night in our old house. A few days later, barely a week after having a c-section, I was home with my newborn, unpacking boxes and taking care of my older girls. We couldn't have done it without family and a faith community who surrounded us, and pitched in. Every night for weeks, meals were delivered to our door. It was an incredible blessing to be on the receiving end of love outpoured from our faith community. And our children got a front row seat to what we read about here in Hebrews 10.

## SET THE PRIORITY
We made it a priority from the beginning to raise our children in the midst of a faith community. Our children are blessed with godly grandparents, aunts, and uncles, but they have also been loved by pastors and children's ministry volunteers and friends who share our faith. Church has always been home – Isabel took her first steps their, Sofia can't wait to help lead worship in her class every Sunday, Josie is comforted by a loving volunteer through her separation anxiety. Taking our kids to church every week isn't always easy. For over a decade I had to get them ready and take them by myself and some weeks I gave up – exactly what this passage in Hebrews warns us not to do. But I recognized the value in our faith community and so I made it a priority to not just attend church, but to value and contribute to my faith community.

## GATHER AND SERVE
Sometimes modeling faith community looks like showing up on Sunday morning, meeting together because it's what God's Word instructs us to do. Sometimes it looks like serving. Sometimes it looks like bringing a meal to a new mom, encouraging her with food and solidarity because I've been there, too. Modeling faith community is all these things and more, trusting that our kids will grow to serve and be served by friends and family who share their faith.

Photo © Dmitry Lobanov

# BABY *Steps*

Bringing an infant to church is a lot of work, whether we bring them to the church nursery, hold them as we participate in an adult service, or sit with them in the nursing mom's room. But making this time a part of your weekly rhythm, committing to meeting regularly with other believers, lays a foundation for your child's spiritual journey. Look around you – the people in your church will come alongside of you to show your child what it means to follow Christ. Make a commitment if you haven't already to participate and invest in your faith community. Find people ahead of you in your journey to guide you along the way. Look for people who follow behind, and spur them on.

## BABY *Bite*

Taking kids to church every week isn't always easy.

## TODDLER *Tips*

Look around you – the people in your church will come alongside of you to show your child what it means to follow Christ. Make a commitment if you haven't already to participate and invest in your faith community.

# TODDLER *Steps*

Bringing a toddler to church has its difficulties – separation anxiety, behavioral challenges, colds that seem to drag on all winter, and a host of other hurdles can challenge your resolve to commit to your faith community. But toddlers also thrive on routine so making faith community a regular rhythm in your weekly schedule will help your toddler become comfortable and learn to look forward to those gatherings. Whether your child participates in their own class, or joins you in gathering with other families, you are modeling the importance of faith community to your child. Surround yourself with those who are ahead of you on the journey so they can guide you along the way, as well as with those who are behind so you can spur them on.

# CHAPTER 51

# Model Accountability

## 📖 MEDITATE

*Therefore confess your sins to each other and pray for each other so that you may be healed. The prayer of a righteous person is powerful and effective.* – James 5:16 (NIV)

Extended passage: James 5:13-18

## ✏️ ANTICIPATE

● When you face a tough decision, who do you seek advice from?

_____

_____

● What friend do you depend on in your parenting journey?

_____

_____

_____

Brian and Brianne played an important role in my life as a husband and a father. Before I had children, my wife Noel worked with Brianne and I worked with Brian. This friendship was as life-giving as it was challenging. When I needed help, Brian was there. When it was time to decorate baby rooms, Brian was there to paint. Brian and Brianne were our friends, confidants, encouragers, co-conspirators, but one of the greatest roles they played was referee. Sometimes you need a life referee. As you face difficult choices and crossroads in your marriage or as a parent, you weigh all of the options and gather all of the information and you need a referee to help you make the call or call a foul. We need someone to come alongside us in the journey and give us wisdom, and provide discernment, encouragement, and accountability.

## ACCOUNTABILITY

It takes courage to embrace accountability because it requires us to confess what is really happening. This is never easy because the pressure to compare, live up to expectations, or be better than everyone around us is overwhelming. Parents are supposed to know everything and do no wrong. We often curate our social media stream to present a perfect picture of our lives that measures up to our expectations.

The truth is we make mistakes. I make them all the time. I made a mistake in my parenting while writing this chapter in the words I spoke to my son Zion and when he wakes up from his nap, I will go and make it right. Moms and dads, it's vital for each of us to establish the kind of accountability freeing us to unashamedly and vulnerably share the raw moments of our lives with others.

Photo © Anna Om

# BABY *Steps*

This week, model accountability by confessing to someone you trust when you've made a mistake as a parent. Some days seem longer than others or more challenging. Your heart, words, attitudes, or actions might not always represent what God desires. When you face these challenges, send a text of confession or call a trusted friend.

## BABY *Bite*

It takes courage to embrace accountability because it requires us to confess what is really happening.

## TODDLER *Tips*

The result of embracing
accountability and prayer is
a life literally exploding
with possibility.

# TODDLER *Steps*

This week, help teach your toddler to accept
responsibility and admit mistakes. Model accountability
for them. Toddlers tell stories they believe are true (my toy
broke the lamp, the dog filled the bathtub with all of my
clothes). This will require your response to be filled with
love, from your words to your facial expressions. Call in
your accountability partner (or referee) when you need to
know if you've gone too far or not far enough.

# CHAPTER 52

# Model Remembrance

## 📖 MEDITATE

*"LORD, I will remember what you did. Yes, I will remember your miracles of long ago."* – Psalm 77:11

Extended passage: Psalm 77:11 (NIV)

## ✏️ ANTICIPATE

● When you hold your baby, what are some things you're reminded of?

_____

_____

● What are some important memories of God at work in your life?

_____

_____

_____

Josie is my fourth and last baby. Each milestone takes me down memory lane for a moment as I remember these moments with her brother and sisters. These memories engage my senses and connect me to moments that happened long ago but feel like just yesterday. Even though Josie doesn't have these memories as her own, I often share them with her, eager to pass them on because they are meaningful to me and I want them to be meaningful to her, too.

## ALTARS OF REMEMBRANCE

In the Old Testament when God would perform a miracle or mighty act of rescue, the Israelites would build an altar to worship God. The altar would stand as a reminder of what God accomplished. As families passed by these altars it prompted stories of what God had done so their children would know who and whose they were. Long gone are the days where altars were built to remind our children of miracles and rescues. *But our children still desperately need to be reminded, and so do we.* Because these reminders anchor our hearts in who God is in the midst of a world that is constantly shifting away from him. These reminders serve as markers along the path that orient us when we lose our way. These reminders point us to the One who is meant to guide us on the straight and narrow path when we struggle to keep going. These markers tell us who and whose we are. It's crucial to be intentional about sharing these reminders with our children. Because someday they will set out on their own and we want them to continue along their faith journey, remembering who God is and what he has done, so they follow him for all of their days.

## PASSING ON THE FAITH

So dear friend, remember God always. Teach your child to remember God always. And as you do, you will pass on a faith that is meaningful to you, faith in a God that is everything to you, faith that your child will carry and pass on to their children, too.

Photo © Ermolaev Alexander

219

# BABY

Babies love looking at faces, especially in the mirror. Sit your child in front of a mirror and read Psalm 77:11 as a blessing over them. Tell them what God has done in your life and theirs. Share miracles that you have seen and experienced. Commit to making this a habit in your home, a regular rhythm where you talk with your child about who God is and what he has done. It can be an informal habit, where you carve out moments of remembrance as they come to mind or as God lays them on your heart. Or they can be more formal traditions, where you plan a time of day or a day each week or month where you sit and share what God has done and is doing in your life. Make these moments a habit so that your child grows to see God as central to you and to your family.

## BABY

Long gone are the days where altars were built to remind our children of miracles and rescues. *But our children still desperately need to be reminded, and so do we.*

Teach your child to remember God always. And as you do, you will pass on a faith that is meaningful to you, faith in a God that is everything to you, faith that your child will carry and pass on to their children, too.

# TODDLER *Steps*

Toddlers love to hear stories of "when they were little." Sit with your child and share photos or stories of when they were smaller, sharing how God blessed you with your child and ways that God has cared for your family. Read Psalm 77:11 as a blessing over them, and briefly share who God is and what he has done. It could be as simple as "God made me and he has blessed me by making me your mom/dad." Commit to making this habit of remembering who God is and what he has done a regular rhythm in your home. Be intentional so that remembrance becomes a habit that is central in your home, teaching your child that God is central to you and your family.

## New! On the Go Family Devotions: Journeying Together

A Devotional for Families with Children Ages 3–10

**Ages 3–10, 224 pages, 5½"x 8½" Paperback, Full Color Illustrations, Retail $16.99**

On The Go Family Devotions: Journeying Together takes the framework introduced in Deuteronomy 6 and applies to the daily life in the modern family. Each devotional gives parents ways to share their faith at home, on the road, when they wake up, and before they go to sleep. Each week, parents will engage in a devotion that centers them in Scripture and creates habits of engaging in casual conversations about God that will propel their child forward in their spiritual journey.

| On the Go: Journeying Together | L50006 | 9781628625011 | $16.99 |

## New! The Children's Rhyming Bible

When a story rhymes, kids want to hear it all the time!

**Ages 3–7, 72 pages, 8"x 7" Hardcover, Full Color Illustrations, Retail $14.99**

Capture and keep your kids' attention with this beloved Children's Rhyming Bible. Featuring joyful illustrations, vivid colors, and a bouncing beat, this beloved Rhyming Bible tells 34 popular Bible stories in an engaging and unforgettable way.

From Creation and Noah's Ark to Jesus' Birth and Resurrection, boys and girls will love the delightful rhymes that will stick in their minds and help them hide God's Word in their hearts. Each Bible story is short, easy-to-read, and stays accurate to the Bible. Perfect for reading aloud to younger children, bedtime stories, or even for older children wanting to read the Bible to themselves.

| The Children's Rhyming Bible | L50004 | 9781628624991 | $14.99 |

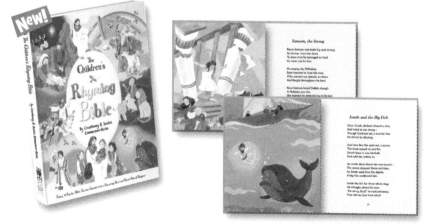

# R⚘SEKiDZ

# BEST-SELLING DEVOTIONALS FOR GIRLS!

## New! God and Me! for Little Ones
My First Devotional for Toddler Girls Ages 2-3

**Ages 2–3, 32 pages, 8"x 8" Hardcover, Full Color Illustrations, Retail $9.99,**

This is the perfect first devotional for little girls ages 2-3. This Read-It-To-Me book helps toddler girls learn about God's love and care. Parents, grandparents and teachers can read the stories aloud to the child. Includes seven stories, each with Bible verse, question, and a prayer. Topics: Helping others, being thankful, trusting God, learning to obey, sharing, and being brave.

| My First Devotional for Toddler Girls | L46841 | 978-1-584111-82-5 | $9.99 |

## New! God and Me!
A Devotional for Girls Ages 4-7

**Ages 4–7, 32 pages, 8"x 8" Hardcover, Full Color Illustrations, Retail $9.99,**

This new devotional for girls ages 4-7 helps them learn about God's love and care. Parents, grandparents and teachers can read the stories aloud to younger children. It includes seven stories, each with Bible verse, question, and a prayer. Topics: Knowing God, being thankful, trusting God, being kind, and God made me special.

| A Devotional for Girls Ages 4-7 | L46837 | 978-1-584111-73-3 | $9.99 |

# R🌹SEKiDZ New for Parents

## New! God and Me! 52 Week Devotional for Girls

**384–386 pages, 6"x 9" Softcover, Full Color Illustrations, Retail $14.99**

This devotional made for girls ages 6–9 and 10-12 covers situations you deal with at school and at home. Enjoy fully illustrated devotions as you are encouraged to rely on God by learning more about Him, His Word, and His plans for your life. Our unique 52-week devotional contains devotions and prayers on Days 1 through 5, and fun activities at the end of the week to reinforce the week's key Scripture memory verse and theme. Each day is designed to help you draw close to God.

| | | | |
|---|---|---|---|
| Ages 6-9 | L46838 | 978-1-584111-77-1 | $14.99 |
| Ages 10-12 | L46839 | 978-1-584111-78-8 | $14.99 |

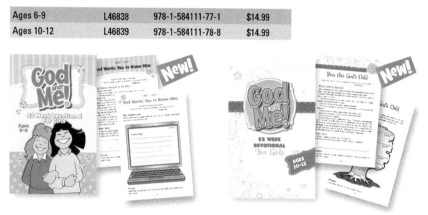

## New! 52 Weekly Devotions for Busy Families

Enjoy having 52 weekly family devotions that you can do in as little as 5 minutes!

**Ages 4–12, 224 pages, 5½"x 7½" Paperback, Full Color Illustrations, Retail $16.99**

You want your children to get to know God better, but how do you do that? Between homework, errands, and extracurricular activities, it's hard to find time to get the whole family together. With such a packed schedule, how can you make room for devotions?

As short as 5 minutes or as long as an hour, the flexible design of this family devotional fits quality time and Bible learning right into your schedule! 52 Weekly Devotions for Busy Families gives you a plan to nurture your children's journey of faith with 5-minute devotionals and optional questions and activities to use throughout the week. If you're busy, just pick one idea. If you have more time, pick several of them! Perfect for families on the go!

| | | | |
|---|---|---|---|
| 52 Weekly Devotions for Busy Families | L50001 | 9781628625080 | $16.99 |